The Random House I

Summer

Annuals

ROGER PHILLIPS
& MARTYN RIX

Research by Peter Barnes, Ruth Grover & Meg Baker
Design by Jill Bryan & Debby Curry

RANDOM HOUSE

Acknowledgements

We would like to thank the following gardens and
suppliers for allowing us to visit them and
photograph their plants:
The Royal Horticultural Society's Garden, Wisley;
The Royal Botanic Gardens, Kew; the University
Botanic Garden, Cambridge; Barnsley House
Garden; Arley Hall; Hidcote Manor; Drummond
Castle Gardens; Tapeley Park; Eccleston Square
Gardens; Herrenhausen; Longwood Gardens;
Wave Hill; Villa Pallavicino; Villa Gamberaia;
Villa Torrigiani; Monet's garden at Giverny; the
Ballymaloe Cookery School Garden; Bosvigo
House, Truro; Thompson and Morgan; Colgrave
Seeds; Sutton Seeds and Fibrex Nurseries.

Among others who have helped in one way or
another we would like to thank: Sheila Bryan;
Jan and Derick Curry; Pamela Egremont;
Marilyn Inglis; Gill Stokoe and Alison Rix.

Random House website address:
www.atrandom.com

Printed in Great Britain
98765432
First U.S. Edition

Color Reproduction by Aylesbury Studios Ltd.
Printed by Butler and Tanner Ltd. Frome, Somerset

Contents

Poppies and cornflowers in a wild flower meadow

Introduction

This book is divided into three main sections using the flowering times of plants as a guide. The earliest begins to flower in spring and continues into early summer. The second group also germinates in cool weather and flowers through the summer. The third group, of subtropical annuals, mostly from Mexico and South America, needs summer heat to germinate, and flowers mainly in late summer and autumn.

Spring annuals include plants like pansies that are planted in autumn and flower from late winter through to early summer. These plants are especially useful for raised beds and pots, excellent grown near paths and near the house where they can be seen from the windows.

The summer group is an important section for any garden. Annuals really come into their own when most shrubs and trees have finished their spring flowering. If well watered, they will give joy and excitement all through the summer months, months that are too hot for other groups of plants to be at their best.

The autumn section contains the plants that flower from late summer through to the first frosts. These are the plants that will bring your garden alive when you return from your summer holidays.

Obviously, these are not hard and fast divisions. Some 'summer' plants can be persuaded to flower earlier if they are grown in pots in a conservatory or cool greenhouse. Others may have their flowering period extended into autumn if they are planted late or taken inside when the winter frosts begin. However, the sections will give some indication of what is at its best in each season, and with careful planning you should be able to have colour in your garden from late winter to the first hard winter frosts.

Getting started

The normal, and of course cheapest, way of making sure you have a good show of annuals in the garden is to grow them from seed. There are two principal ways of doing this: the first is to scatter the seed on the flowerbed and lightly rake it in. Some annuals, such as poppies, grow very well from seed when just scattered like this. This method has the great advantage of allowing the plants to grow as they want – thus giving a natural or wild feeling to the garden. The second method is to grow the seed in a seed tray, and plant out the seedlings when they reach sufficient maturity to be handled. This is a more reliable way of achieving good germination, and has the added advantage of giving you control over how you position the young plants to achieve the effect you want.

There is a third way, which is to spend a little more money and buy young plants at your local nursery or plant centre. To some extent the method you choose will be dictated by the nature of the plants, and we have tried to give some indication of this in the Planting Help section that accompanies each entry.

Colour

Choosing your colour scheme is most important with annuals, as many of them have strong colours that, although bright and striking in a garden as individuals, may look very odd together. The only rule is to think about what you want to achieve. If you want a cool and subtle effect, think first of the whites and blues. However, if you feel that

you have had enough of all this tasteful gardening, go for bold yellows and reds. You can also vary your garden scheme from year to year: be loud one year and subtle the next. Which ever way you do it, it will always be more effective if you overdo it!

Buying seed

There are two ways of buying seeds: either visit your local nursery or plant centre and browse through the seed packets that will be on display, or write away for a catalogue from one of the principal seed merchants. In many ways this second alternative is the more satisfactory as you can sit at home and have fun devising new ideas and colour combinations on cold wet days in winter. You will also be able to keep up with the ever-changing range of varieties on offer, as the seed merchants are constantly trying to improve on the quality of their products. They have moved with the times and you can now order by fax, E-mail or telephone.

Pansies, pelargoniums, impatiens, lobelia and fuchsias in pots in St Ives

Viola 'Bowles's Black'

Heartsease *Viola tricolor*

Viola 'Prince John' with *Muscari* 'Blue Spike'

'Yesterday, Today and Tomorrow' with flowers that open almost white, ageing to lavender blue

Pansies & Violas

Pansies and violas are some of the easiest and most useful dwarf annuals for flowering in spring and early summer. They have long been cultivated and hybridized, using the wild British native *Viola tricolor*, crossed with other European species. Modern annual cultivars fall uneasily into two groups, pansies with large flowers, usually with a dark face or centre, and violas with smaller, plain-coloured flowers. In addition there is a large group of small-flowered perennial violas which are grown from cuttings.

Heartsease *Viola tricolor*   Native to much of Europe, including the British Isles and has been grown in gardens for centuries. A spreading annual or biennial plant that grows to 6in (15cm) tall, and produces yellow and purple flowers ¾in (2cm) wide in spring and summer. Many of the modern small-flowered viola cultivars have a much wider colour range: **'Prince John'** has small, bright yellow flowers; in the old variety **'Bowles's Black'** they are virtually black with a tiny yellow eye.

Pansies *Viola × wittrockiana*   These are of hybrid origin and may be grown as annuals, biennials or short-lived perennials. With much bigger flowers than Heartsease, they have rounded blooms 2–4in (5–10cm) wide, in white, blue, purple, yellow, orange and red shades. There is a range of bicoloured varieties and many have a large central blotch of deep purple. They flower from spring to summer or, in the case of winter-flowering

Pansies and the shrubby *Convolvulus cneorum* in pots

pansies, from the earliest fine days of winter through to spring. They are hardy to −10°F (−23°C), US zones 6–9.

PLANTING HELP   Seeds are sown in late winter to flower in summer, or in summer to flower the following winter. They like a fertile, well-drained soil and a position in sun or partial shade. Regular dead-heading is necessary to prolong flowering and helps to keep the plants tidy.

Pansies

Pansy 'Universal Light Blue' with *Narcissus* 'Hawera' at Kew

Limnanthes douglasii var. *sulphurea*

Limnanthes douglasii Poached-egg Plant

Nemophila maculata

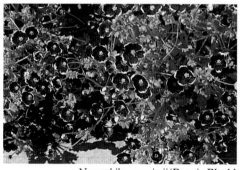

Nemophila menziesii 'Pennie Black'

Phacelia 'Tropical Surf'

Limnanthes

Limnanthes douglasii Poached-egg Plant
Native to the SW United States and introduced to
Europe in the early 19th century. It is a bushy,
spreading annual that grows to about 8in (20cm)
tall, with attractive divided, vivid green foliage and
bowl-shaped white flowers 1in (2.5cm) wide, each
with a large central zone of bright yellow (or
uniformly yellow in **var. *sulphurea***), produced
over a long period in the summer and autumn. It
is fragrant and rich in nectar and very attractive to
bees. Hardy to 10°F (−12°C), US zones 8–10.
Once introduced to a garden it will often sow itself
from year to year. The Poached-egg Plant is very
easy to grow and makes an excellent edging for the
front of a border or a path.

PLANTING HELP   Sow seeds where they are
to flower, in autumn or early spring, preferably in
an open, sunny position in fertile, well-drained but
fairly moist soil. It is a trouble-free plant.

Nemophila

An attractive genus of small annuals, mostly from
California. These are some of the easiest and
quickest annuals to flower from a planting in
spring, or in mild areas they can overwinter and so
build up larger plants. Both species are hardy to
10°F (−12°C), US zones 8–10 or somewhat lower.

PLANTING HELP   Both species like fertile,
well-drained soil in a sunny or partially sunny
position which is not liable to dry out. Sow seeds
where they are to flower in early spring or autumn;
once established, they will often sow themselves
from year to year. Greenfly may be a problem.

Phacelia 'Tropical Surf' with pink lobelia

Nemophila maculata   Native to California, where it is known as Five-spot, and first cultivated in Europe in the mid-19th century. It is a bushy annual that grows up to 12in (30cm) tall with bowl-shaped white flowers which have darker veins and a prominent violet spot at the tip of each petal. Each flower is about 1½in (4cm) wide and the small leaves are divided into blunt lobes.

Nemophila menziesii Baby Blue-eyes
Also from California and a little smaller than *N. maculata*, with long-stalked flowers that are sky blue, with a pale blue or white centre.

Nemophila menziesii
Baby Blue-eyes

Nemophila menziesii 'Pennie Black'
A striking selection with almost black flowers, narrowly edged with white. Other colour selections are sometimes seen.

Phacelia campanularia

Phacelia

Phacelia campanularia   A bushy annual that grows to 12in (30cm) tall, it is native to California and was introduced to Europe in the late 19th century. The bell-shaped flowers are 1in (2.5cm) wide, dark gentian blue with a white centre, and appear from late spring to summer above the oval, dark green leaves. Forms with pure white flowers are also grown. Hardy to 20°F (−6°C), US zones 9–10. **Phacelia 'Tropical Surf'** has larger flowers of the typical rich blue, with a white speckled centre.

PLANTING HELP   Sow seeds in the open garden in autumn or spring. It likes a fertile, well-drained soil and full sun.

Godetias

Clarkia amoena and cultivars Usually grown as Godetias, these are native to California. They have single or double flowers in a range of colours, usually shades of pink, purple or striped. The cup-shaped flowers are freely produced over a long period in the summer, making a wonderful display in a sunny border. Very good for cutting and can also be grown as flowering pot plants in a greenhouse. They grow 12–18in (30–45cm) tall, and are hardy to 10°F (−12°C), US zones 8–10.

Godetia

PLANTING HELP Sow seed outside where the plant is to flower from March to June. Thin seedlings 6–9in (15–23cm) apart. The plants will grow in any well-drained soil and prefer a sunny, open position.

Bird's Eyes *Gilia tricolor*

Gilia capitata

Clarkias

Clarkia pulchella This easily grown native of western North America grows 12–15in (30–40cm) tall and has thin spikes of colourful double or semi-double flowers for a long period over the summer. The petals are generally narrow, widening towards their apex. The flowers are various shades of pink, lilac or white and can be used to add colour among shrubs as well as in borders or containers. They are also good for cutting. Hardy to 20°F (−6°C), US zones 9–10.

Clarkia 'Double Salmon'

Godetia 'Satin Pink'

Godetias on a Cornish 'Hedge'

PLANTING HELP   Seeds can be sown in the spring *in situ*. They need well-drained, fairly rich soil and a sunny or partially shaded position. Seedlings should be thinned to 12in (30cm) apart. For earlier flowering plants for containers, sow seeds in late summer or autumn and overwinter in a greenhouse. Regular dead-heading will prolong the flowering season.

Gilia

Annual gilias are easy to grow with attractive, finely cut foliage and colourful flowers. They are particularly valuable for their long flowering period, lasting from early summer into the autumn. They are generally free from pests and diseases and need little attention once established.

PLANTING HELP   Seeds can be sown in spring where they are to flower, ⅛in (3mm) deep. The seedlings should be thinned out to 12in (30cm) apart. Alternatively, the sowing can be done in late summer or early autumn, with a final thinning of the seedlings in the spring. Container plants for flowering in a conservatory or greenhouse in winter and early spring should be sown in late summer to early autumn and watered sparingly. Gilias will grow in any well-drained soil and need a sunny position.

Gilia capitata   Native from British Columbia to California and New Mexico, this plant grows 36–40in (90–100cm) tall and is very suitable for cutting. All summer it produces rounded heads of lavender blue flowers on slender stems with mid-green, feathery foliage. Hardy to 20°F (–6°C), US zones 9–10.

Bird's Eyes *Gilia tricolor*   The erect branching stems of this plant grow to 15in (40cm) tall with mid-green foliage, consisting of thin 1½in (4cm) long leaves divided into narrow segments. From early summer this species produces clusters of pale or deep violet blue and white flowers. Each flower is about ½in (1.5cm) or more wide and has a short orange yellow tube. Hardy to 20°F (–6°C), US zones 9–10. *Gilia tricolor* is wild in grassy places in California and is a very pretty annual for any sunny border. It can also be grown in containers.

Clarkia pulchella 'Mixed Royal Bouquet' (*left*) and 'Snowlake' (*right*)

Eschscholzia californica self-sown in Australia

Eschscholzia californica 'Sundew'

Eschscholzia californica 'Alba'

California Poppy

Eschscholzia californica An herbaceous perennial native to western North America, but most often grown as an annual. The wild species grows to 2ft (60cm) tall and, in late spring and summer, produces four-petalled, 3in (8cm) wide poppy flowers in deep orange or yellow. The foliage is an attractive blue green colour. Many cultivars have now been produced with flowers in colours ranging from pale lemon to strong pink and mauve, with doubles and frilly semi-doubles available, and generally smaller, only growing about 1ft (30cm) tall. *Eschscholzia californica* is well known and reliable as an annual, easily grown in almost any garden with plenty of sun and is sometimes naturalized in warm countries. Hardy to 10°F (−12°C), US zones 8–10.

PLANTING HELP Sow seed outdoors where the plant is to flower in autumn or mid-spring. Repeated sowings will give a successive show of flowers. They will grow in any well-drained soil and need a position in full sun.

CALIFORNIA POPPIES

'Ballerina Mixed'   'Cherry Ripe'

'Purple Violet'

'Milky White'

California poppies from Eccleston Square, ⅔ life-size

Eschscholzia californica 'Apricot Flame'

Eschscholzia californica 'Thai Silk Rose Chiffon'

Eschscholzia californica by a path at Tapeley Park

Diascia 'Blackthorn Apricot' at Wisley

Nemesia strumosa, mixed colours, with *Nemesia versicolor* 'Blue Gem' at Wisley

Diascia 'Paula'

Nemesia 'Triumph Red'

Southern Hemisphere Perennials

The plants shown on these pages are short-lived perennials, usually grown as annuals, from the Southern Hemisphere. They are often sold as small plants in the spring and will flower throughout the summer, provided they have fertile soil and ample water. Seed may be sown in spring.

PLANTING HELP All these plants prefer light, moist, but well-drained soil and a sunny position. Regular dead-heading will prolong the flowering period. Take cuttings of tender perennials in early autumn and overwinter them in a frame or greenhouse, keeping them rather dry.

Alonsoa

A small genus of short-lived perennials or shrubs from South America. The species usually cultivated, *Alonsoa warscewiczii*, is distinct for its intense bright scarlet flowers, produced through the summer on stems to 1ft (30cm) tall. The variety 'Peachy Keen' has paler flowers. In **'Coral'** the peach flowers are stippled with red. Both are hardy to 20°F (−6°C), US zones 9–10, for short periods.

Alonsoa warscewiczii 'Coral'

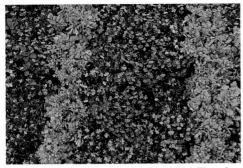

Lobelia erinus 'Cambridge Blue' with Feverfew

Lobelia with petunias, pelargoniums and pansies

Diascia

There are around 50 species of annual and perennial *Diascia* native to South Africa, and several species and many named varieties are now well established in cultivation. From early summer to mid-autumn they produce slender spikes of delicate flowers on plants 12–18in (30–45cm) tall. Cultivars are available with flowers in various shades of pink and white, some with a tinge of orange. They make very good container plants, as well as being suited to a sheltered position in a sunny border. Although they will tolerate temperatures down to 10°F (–12°C), US zones 8–10 if protected from wet in winter, they cannot be treated as reliably hardy.

Nemesia

Nemesia strumosa An annual native to the southwest coast of South Africa and introduced to Europe at the end of the 19th century. Its two-lipped flowers, 1in (2.5cm) wide, range in colour from white to yellow, pink, purple and blue. Hardy to 20°F (–6°C), US zones 9–10. **'Triumph Red'** has rich crimson flowers. ***Nemesia versicolor*** has flowers of blue and white, red and white or plain blue in **'Blue Gem'**.

Scaevola

Scaevola aemula A tender perennial usually grown as an annual with a trailing habit that makes it ideal for hanging baskets and other containers. It is native to south and SE Australia and was probably first introduced to Europe in the 19th century, although it has only been commonly grown in recent years. The stems can trail to 2ft (60cm) or longer and blue or blue purple flowers about 1in (2.5cm) across, with the petals arranged in a fan shape, are produced from early summer to autumn, even into winter in mild

areas. Hardy to 32°F (0°C), US zone 10. It can be treated as a perennial if overwintered in a frost-free greenhouse.

Lobelia

Lobelia erinus Native to South Africa, this tender, trailing perennial is usually grown as an annual. In summer it produces a long succession of small flowers. Numerous selections, either bushy or trailing, are available in many shades of blue, pink and violet as well as white. There are also double-flowered forms and some varieties with bronze foliage. They can be used for bedding and edging, and the trailing varieties are popular container plants, used particularly in hanging baskets. Lobelias can be grown in any zone but will be killed by the first frost.

PLANTING HELP Sow seed indoors in warmth in late winter. They should go uncovered into a light seed compost. The seedlings need to be hardened off gradually and can be planted out at the end of May. They prefer a humus-rich, moist soil and a position in full sun or partial shade. They need feeding occasionally to maintain good flowering.

Scaevola aemula 'Blue Fan'

Portulaca grandiflora 'Sundial Peppermint'

Portulaca grandiflora 'Cloudbeater Mixed'

Livingstone Daisy *Dorotheanthus bellidiformis*

Brachyscome iberidifolia

Portulaca

Portulaca grandiflora
Rose Moss   This annual is native to South America and was introduced to Europe in the early 19th century. It forms a spreading plant 4–6in (10–15cm) tall, with awl-shaped fleshy leaves and silky textured flowers, 1–2in (2.5–5cm) wide, in shades of rose red, pink, yellow and white. Hardy to 32°F (0°C), US zone 10. Some double-flowered selections like **'Sunstate White'** have semi-double, white flowers. **'Sundial Peppermint'** has semi-double white flowers striped and flecked with rose pink. Portulaca is an easily grown and colourful plant for any dry, sunny position.

Portulaca

PLANTING HELP   Seeds are sown in a warm greenhouse or propagator in early spring and planted out when the danger of frost has passed. It flowers most freely in a nutrient-poor soil and full sun.

Swan River Daisy

Brachyscome iberidifolia (often mis-spelled *Brachycome*)   This annual is native to south and west Australia and was introduced to Europe in the mid-19th century. A bushy or spreading annual that grows to 12in (30cm) tall, with lacy

Mixed Swan River daisies

foliage and blue, purple, pinkish or white daisies 1in (2.5cm) wide, throughout the summer and autumn. Hardy to 10°F (−12°C), US zones 8–10. **'Blue Star'** and **'White Splendour'** are two good selections, but a massed planting of mixed colours can also be effective.

PLANTING HELP   The Swan River daisy enjoys a sunny position in well-drained soil and is also ideal for use in containers. Seeds are sown in warmth in early spring and planted out when all danger of frost has passed.

Felicia

Felicia amelloides   Native to South Africa and introduced to Europe in the mid-18th century, this *Felicia* is a tender perennial sub-shrub that grows to 2ft (60cm) tall, but is most often grown as an annual, flowering throughout the summer and autumn. Slender stems carry light or deep blue daisies with yellow centres, ¾–2in (2–5cm) wide, well above the dark green, ovate leaves. Hardy to 32°F (0°C), US zone 10. As well as the typical blue form, there is a good white one of compact habit, and the large-flowered 'Santa Anita'. A sport, 'Santa Anita Variegated' has leaves marked with creamy white.

PLANTING HELP   Seeds are sown in warmth in early spring and hardened off before planting out in late spring. Cuttings of the stem tips can be rooted in late summer for use the following year. It needs a well-drained soil and a sunny position. Regular dead-heading will prolong flowering.

Livingstone Daisy

Dorotheanthus bellidiformis
(syn. *Mesembryanthemum criniflorum*)   Native to South Africa and introduced to Europe in the late 19th century. It forms a low spreading plant to 4in (10cm) tall, with fleshy oblong leaves covered with tiny glistening cells like frost. The daisy-like flowers, about 1½in (4cm) wide, open only in bright sunlight. Colours range from white to yellow, salmon, pink and magenta red as well as unusual pastel shades. Hardy to 32°F (0°C), US zone 10. Good mixtures are available, giving colour throughout the summer.

PLANTING HELP   Seeds sown in early spring will need warmth to germinate, and should be hardened off before planting out in late spring. It should have a rather poor soil in full sun. The foliage is often damaged by slugs. The flowers need full sun or warmth to open.

Felicia amelloides 'Santa Cruz'

Livingstone Daisy on a Cornish 'Hedge' in Rinsey

Gazania 'Daybreak Bronze' and 'Daybreak Yellow'

Gazania 'Chansonette Pink'

Osteospermum 'Silver Sparkler'

Arctotis

Arctotis is a small genus of around 50 species, native to southern Africa, generally represented in the garden by hybrids such as **'Raspberry'**, which were formerly called *Veridio-arctotis*. Although more or less perennial, they are usually treated as half-hardy annuals. In summer they bear brightly coloured daisy-like flowers on stems up to 15in (40cm) tall. Not hardy, only surviving down to 32°F (0°C), US zone 10, but they make very showy border plants in mild climates.

PLANTING HELP Sow seed indoors in late spring and plant out after all risk of frost has passed. They need well-drained, leafy soil and should have a sunny position.

Dimorphotheca

Star of the Veldt *Dimorphotheca sinuata* Native to South Africa, this spreading plant grows to 1ft (30cm) tall and usually wider. In spring and summer it produces daisy-like flowers in shades of yellow or orange, which make a beautiful display in a sunny border. Hardy to 20°F (–6°C), US zones 9–10.

PLANTING HELP Sow seed outside where the plant is to flower from April to June. Repeated sowings will give a successive show of flowers. They will grow in any well-drained soil and must have a position in full sun.

Osteospermum

Osteospermum is a genus of half-hardy and tender perennials and annuals, native to South Africa. Most of the perennial garden varieties are derived from *Osteospermum jucundum* and *O. ecklonis*, which were introduced to Europe during the 19th century. They vary from low-growing plants, 4–8in (10–20cm) tall with rooting stems, to bushy upright ones, 18–24in (45–60cm) tall. All have aromatic leaves and a profusion of white, light yellow, pink or purple daisies 2–3in (5–8cm) wide, borne throughout the summer and into autumn. The disk in the centre of the flower is often a contrasting dark colour and the backs of the petals may be blue or purple. Many are hardy to 20°F (–6°C), US zones 9–10, but a few will stand lower temperatures. Recently, a few cultivars with variegated foliage have been introduced, such as **'Silver Sparkler'**.

PLANTING HELP All these plants enjoy a position in full sun and should have a well-drained, fertile soil. Seed of the annual sorts is

Osteospermum 'Stardust'

Arctotis 'Raspberry' in a garden near Los Angeles

sown under glass at 60–65°F (15–18°C) in early spring, the seedlings being hardened off before planting out in late May. Removing the old flower heads will help to prolong the flowering season.

Gazania

The garden hybrid *Gazanias* are derived from South African species, introduced to Europe in the 18th century. Although often perennials, they may be treated as half-hardy annuals, and numerous hybrid series are available. In summer they produce a succession of large, showy daisy flowers in a wide range of hot colours, many with darker centres, on stems to 9in (23cm) tall. The foliage is often a silvery green. Hardy to 20°F (−6°C), US zones 9–10. Gazanias are showy plants for a dry, sheltered, sunny border or for use in containers.

PLANTING HELP   Sow seed indoors in early spring. They need a temperature of 65–68°F (18–20°C) to germinate. The seedlings should be hardened off gradually and planted out after all risk of frost has passed. They will grow in any well-drained soil and need a position in full sun. The flowers may fail to open on dull days or during a cool spell of weather.

Star of the Veldt *Dimorphotheca sinuata* with *Nemesia versicolor* 'Blue Gem'

Pericallis × *hybrida*, an old variety in California

Cinerarias

Pericallis × **hybrida** A group of hybrids between species native to the Azores, Madeira and the Canary Islands. Growing 10–18in (25–45cm) tall, they form bushy plants with oval or heart-shaped leaves and clusters af daisy-like flowers 1–3in (2.5–8cm) wide. Hardy to 20°F (–6°C), US zones 9–10. Originally purple, cinerarias are now available in shades of pink, red, blue, magenta and white, and some forms have two-tone flowers. Although the old varieties are perennial, the modern cultivars are most often treated as annuals, and are valuable for flowering in winter and early spring. **'Brilliant'** is a mixture with large flowers in various colours.

PLANTING HELP Seeds are sown in warmth in spring, to flower the following autumn; if greenhouse-grown, they can be sown in summer to flower the following winter or spring. They need a well-drained fertile soil in partial sun, and under glass should have shade from the strongest sun. Removing old flowers will help to extend the flowering season.

Sanvitalia

Creeping Zinnia *Sanvitalia procumbens*
A spreading plant which is native to Mexico. It reaches only 6in (15cm) tall but can form mats up to 18in (45cm) wide. From early summer to early autumn small daisy-like flowers are produced, with bright yellow petals and black centres. *S. procumbens* makes a good edging plant for paths or borders, and can also be used in rock gardens. Hardy to 10°F (–12°C), US zones 8–10.

PLANTING HELP Sow seed outside where the plant is to flower in autumn or spring. Thinning of autumn-sown seedlings should be left until spring. This plant likes a light, well-drained soil and a position in full sun.

Cineraria 'Brilliant' at Wisley

Creeping Zinnia *Sanvitalia procumbens*

Sanvitalia 'Gold Braid'

CINERARIAS

Cinerarias used as winter bedding plants in Sintra, Portugal

Modern cinerarias at Wisley in December

Convolvulus tricolor 'Blue Ensign' with the red vetch *Hedysarum*

Consolida ambigua 'Frosted Sky'

Convolvulus

Convolvulus tricolor 'Blue Ensign'
This easy-to-grow bushy plant adds colour to beds or containers. Up to 15in (40cm) tall, it bears flowers, 2in (5cm) wide, a strong purple blue with white centres and a golden yellow eye. Flowering time varies – early spring in warm areas such as California, summer in the north. Hardy to 20°F (–6°C), US zones 9–10. Native to southern Europe and North Africa.

PLANTING HELP Outdoors, seeds can be sown ½in (1.5cm) deep where they are to flower, from March to May. Seedlings should be thinned to 9in (23cm) apart. Seed sown indoors in March will yield plants that can be hardened off and planted out in May. They need well-drained soil and a sunny or partially shaded position. Regular dead-heading will extend the season of the short-lived flowers.

Adonis

Pheasant's Eye *Adonis aestivalis* An attractive plant for midsummer colour in a sunny or partially shaded border, *Adonis aestivalis* has feathery, bright green foliage on branched stems that grow to 18in (45cm) tall. From June to August blood red, cup-shaped flowers grow at the ends of the stems and branches. Native to central and southern Europe. Hardy to 10°F (–12°C), US zones 8–10. *Adonis annua*, a rare cornfield weed in S England and Europe, is very similar, but has slightly smaller seeds.

PLANTING HELP Sow seed in autumn or spring in sandy soil in sun. Water well until flowering begins.

Larkspur

Annual Delphinium *Consolida ambigua* (syn. *Delphinium ajacis*) Larkspurs are closely related to perennial delphiniums but are generally shorter with smaller flowers. *Consolida ambigua* is native to the Mediterranean region, is fully hardy and very suitable for cottage gardens. The free-branching plants produce flowers in varying shades of blue, pink or white from early to late summer. *Consolida ambigua* grows 1–3ft (30–90cm) tall. **'Frosted Sky'** is easy to grow, reaches 12–18in (30–45cm) and is particularly good for cutting and drying. Hardy to 0°F (–18°C), US zones 7–10.

PLANTING HELP Seed may be sown outdoors, ¼in (0.5cm) deep, from early spring to early summer, or under cloches in autumn.

Pheasant's Eye *Adonis aestivalis*

Annual Larkspur *Consolida ambigua* mixed colours

Calendula officinalis 'Apricot Bon Bon'

Larkspur prefers well-drained soil and a sunny, sheltered position. In dry weather it requires regular watering. Plants should be spaced 1–1½ft (30–45cm) apart. Its leaves are prone to powdery mildew in dry weather. Dead-heading will prolong its flowering. **Note:** the seeds are poisonous.

Calendula

Pot Marigold *Calendula officinalis*   This is native to central and southern Europe and Asia, and is cultivated as a garden plant all over the world. It has branched stems on which, from June until the first frosts, it bears yellow flowers with numerous, brightly coloured petals. Hardy to 10°F (−12°C), US zones 8–10. The species has given rise to a large number of cultivars with flower colours ranging from cream to deep orange, with double and semi-double blooms available. They are all very easy to grow and reach 12–30in (30–75cm) tall. They make excellent border plants and are very good for cutting. They will also do well in containers.

PLANTING HELP   Sow seed outside where the plant is to flower in September or April. Thinning of autumn-sown seedlings should be left until spring. They can also be started off indoors in March and planted out after the last frost, and should then flower in May. Pot marigolds will grow in any well-drained soil and prefer a position in full sun, but will tolerate partial shade. They are susceptible to mildew in dry but humid weather.

Calendula officinalis 'Touch of Red'

Silene coeli-rosa 'Royal Celebration'

Silene coeli-rosa at Sutton's seed trials near Torquay

Anagallis

Anagallis monellii This perennial, native to southern Europe, is usually grown as a half-hardy annual and belongs to a small genus of low-growing annuals and perennials. It forms a low mat to 6in (15cm) tall, with small, oval, dark green leaves and vivid, deep blue, or sometimes red or pink flowers ¾in (2cm) wide. Hardy to 20°F (–6°C), US zones 9–10. An effective edging for a border, it can also be used on a rock garden.

PLANTING HELP Seeds are sown in early spring in pots in a cold frame. Alternatively, tip cuttings may be taken in summer. It enjoys a fertile, well-drained sandy soil in full sun. I have seen masses of it growing on sand dunes near Jerez in the south of Spain.

Corn Cockle

Agrostemma githago Native to the Mediterranean region, this plant used to be found as a common cornfield weed throughout Europe before the widespread introduction of modern herbicides. It has long narrow leaves on thin downy stems 2–3ft (60–90cm) tall, and a slightly lax habit of growth. An easily grown cottage garden flower, corn cockle blooms freely all summer with 2in (5cm) flowers, plum pink fading to white at the centres. Hardy to 10°F (–12°C), US zones 8–10, and the flowers are quite resistant to wind and rain.

PLANTING HELP Sow the seeds in spring where they are to flower. They will grow in any well-drained garden soil and like a position in full sun. Seed can also be sown in late summer or early autumn for overwintering, and the plants will self-seed freely. Dead-head regularly to prolong the flowering season. **Note:** the seeds of *Agrostemma* are poisonous if eaten.

Toadflax

The species most often grown as garden annuals are cultivars of *Linaria maroccana* and *L. reticulata*, both native to the southern Mediterranean and North Africa. From early summer to September they bear small snapdragon flowers in bright colours with contrasting throats. Some are sold as mixtures of colours, others, such as **'Gold'** as single shades. They are very easy to grow, make useful border fillers and are good for cutting. They grow 6–12in (15–30cm) tall. Hardy to 10°F (–12°C), US zones 8–10. **Note:** all parts of the plants are poisonous.

PLANTING HELP Sow seed outside where the plant is to flower in spring, and also autumn in mild winter areas. Seedlings should be thinned to 6in (15cm) apart. They like a well-drained soil and a position in full sun. They will self-seed freely.

Anagallis monellii

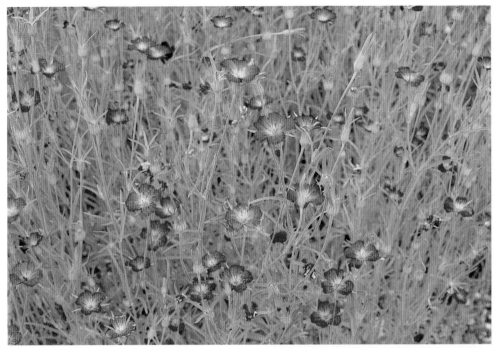

Corn Cockle *Agrostemma githago*

Silene

Silene, Campion or often called Catchfly, because of the sticky stems of many of the species, is a large genus of 500 species, mainly perennials, found throughout the world.

PLANTING HELP   Sow seed outside where the plant is to flower in September or April. The plants need well-drained soil and are equally happy in a sunny or partially shaded position.

Silene coeli-rosa (syn. *Viscaria elegans*)   The cultivars bear flowers in various shades of white, pink or purple and are available in single colours or mixtures, such as **'Royal Celebration'**. They grow up to 15in (40cm) tall and are good for cutting. Hardy to 10°F (−12°C), US zones 8–10.

Silene pendula 'Peach Blossom'   A lower-growing plant, reaching only 6in (15cm) tall but spreading to 12in (30cm) wide. It has double flowers that open from deep pink buds and mature through salmon pink to white. It makes a good edging plant. The flowers are often damaged by wet weather.

Silene pendula 'Peach Blossom'

Linaria maroccana 'Gold'

Poppies

Papaver rhoeas 'Rev. Wilks' mixed

Poppies are among the most easily grown annuals and one of the few cornfield weeds which are still familiar, the seeds surviving many years beneath the soil, and soon appearing in areas which have not been sprayed.

PLANTING HELP   Sow the seeds in spring where they are to flower. Put in sticks for support before the first flowers open.

Papaver rhoeas   The field poppy is a familiar sight in disturbed soil in much of Britain and Europe and was formerly a major weed in cornfields. An erect annual, it can grow up to 2ft (60cm) tall, with narrow lobed leaves and long-stalked scarlet flowers 2–3in (5–8cm) wide. Various selections have been made, of which the Shirley poppies are best-known, with both single and double flowers in many shades from red to pink and white. They were raised by the Rev. W. Wilks, vicar of Shirley, near Croydon, England, in the late 19th century and have been selected further to contain more pastel shades.

Papaver rhoeas **'Mother of Pearl'** (syn. 'Fairy Wings')   A selection with single flowers in soft shades of pink, peach, lilac grey and mauve.

***Papaver commutatum* 'Ladybird'**   Native to the Caucasus, Iran, Turkey and Crete, this attractive annual has been grown in Europe since the mid-19th century. Growing up to 1½ft (45cm) tall, it has narrow, deeply lobed leaves and solitary, bowl-shaped flowers about 3in (8cm) wide. The four petals are a vivid crimson, each with a large square black blotch near the base. Hardy to 0°F (−18°C), US zones 7–10.

Opium and field poppies in Monet's garden at Giverny

'Mother of Pearl'

FIELD POPPIES

Papaver rhoeas, the field poppy growing wild in Suffolk

Papaver commutatum 'Ladybird'

Field poppies with corn cockle

ICELAND POPPIES

Iceland Poppy *Papaver nudicaule*

Iceland Poppy *Papaver nudicaule*
Native to subarctic regions, from which it was
introduced to Europe in the mid-18th century. A
perennial that grows to 12in (30cm) tall with a tuft
of lobed basal leaves and leafless stems, each
bearing a solitary bowl-shaped white or lemon
yellow flower. The many cultivated selections have
flowers up to 5in (12cm) wide in beautiful shades
of orange, yellow, pink and red, as well as white.
Some grow to 18in (45cm) tall. Although strictly
perennial, Iceland poppies are usually short-lived
and grown as biennials. Hardy to
−40°F (−40°C), US zones 3–8.

PLANTING HELP
Sow seeds in spring where
they are to flower or in
containers. They
should be
thinned out if
necessary
and like a
fertile but
well-drained
soil in a sunny
position.

Iceland
Poppies

Papaver somniferum in Australia

Opium Poppy *Papaver somniferum* in Eccleston Square

Opium Poppy *Papaver somniferum*   The opium poppy is of uncertain origin and has been cultivated for centuries. It is a stiffly erect annual that grows to 4ft (1.2m) tall and has smooth blue grey leaves. The familiar forms found in gardens lack any significant toxic content. The bowl-shaped flowers of the wild type are up to 5in (12cm) wide, with four mauve petals blotched with purple at the base. There are many cultivated forms, with single and double flowers that may be white, mauve, pink or red; some forms have fringed petals. Hardy to 0°F (−18°C), US zones 7–10.

PLANTING HELP
Sow the seeds in spring where they are to flower. Remove dead flower heads before they seed to prolong flowering and prevent the plants becoming a nuisance by self-seeding. Self-seeding may get out of hand if every flower is allowed to go to seed.

Single
Papaver somniferum
mixed

Pink Hawksbeard *Crepis rubra*

Crepis

Pink Hawksbeard *Crepis rubra* This native of the Mediterranean flourishes in dry soil and rockeries. It is easy to grow and bears a mass of dandelion-like flowers in the summer. These are usually pale pink, but a white-flowered variety is also available. The plants grow up to 12in (30cm) tall and have rosettes of leaves and slender stems. Hardy to 10°F (–12°C), US zones 8–10.

PLANTING HELP   Sow seed outside where the plant is to flower in spring. It needs a well-drained soil and a position in full sun. Pink Hawksbeard will self-seed freely.

Bells of Ireland *Molucella laevis*

Gypsophila

Gypsophila elegans   Derived from a species native to the eastern Mediterranean, this plant grows up to 18in (45cm) tall. It is an easily grown plant and bears a profusion of sprays of small flowers from late spring to early autumn. It makes a valuable addition to borders or containers, and is much used in flower arrangments. **'Covent Garden'** is a popular white-flowered form, very suitable for cutting. As the name suggests, 'Giant White' has white flowers which are larger than those of other cultivars, up to ¾in (2cm) across. Hardy to 10°F (–12°C), US zones 8–10.

PLANTING HELP   Seed should be sown outdoors in late spring or early autumn where it is to flower. This plant likes a sunny position and well-drained, preferably alkaline, soil.

Gypsophila 'Covent Garden'

Molucella

Bells of Ireland *Molucella laevis*   Native to W Asia where it grows in cornfields and cultivated in Europe since the 16th century. An annual that grows to 2ft (60cm) tall with small two-lipped white or pale mauve flowers that are borne in late

Single-flowered *Nigella damascena*

Nigella hispanica

summer, in whorls on a spike to 1ft (30cm) long. Each flower sits within a large, slightly spiny, bowl-shaped, pale green calyx. Hardy to 0°F (−18°C), US zones 7–10. The shell-like green calyx persists long after the small flowers fade and the stems are useful for drying for winter decoration.

PLANTING HELP   Seeds may be sown in a warm greenhouse 60°F (15°C) in early spring, pricked out and hardened off before planting out in late spring. Seeds can also be sown in the open ground in April. It likes a fertile, well-drained soil in full sun.

Love-in-a-mist

Love-in-a-mist (*Nigella damascena*) has bluish flowers, surrounded by a ruff of narrow leaves. The seed pods, which are one of their most distinct features, enlarge greatly as they ripen, and have 2–14 horns. They can be dried and used in winter arrangements. *Nigella sativa* (*not illustrated*) provides black aromatic seeds which are used to flavour bread.

PLANTING HELP   Seeds of *Nigella* are usually sown where they are to flower, either in autumn or in early spring, and thinned out as

necessary. They should have an open, sunny position. If the plants are left in the ground after flowering, they frequently self-seed.

Love-in-a-mist *Nigella damascena*   A well-known cottage garden annual native to southern Europe and North Africa, and introduced to gardens by the 16th century. Each flower is 1¼–1½in (3–4cm) wide and sits within a large ruff of leaves with thread-like segments, similar to the leaves. The inflated seed pods are good for drying for winter decoration. *Nigella damascena* is available in several named selections, with white, pink, pale or deep blue flowers, as well as some dwarf forms not exceeding 10in (25cm) tall. Some varieties have a single row of petals, others such as 'Miss Jekyll' have 2 or more rows. It is hardy to 0°F (−18°C), US zones 7–10 or lower.

Nigella hispanica   Native to southern France and Spain, this bushy annual was introduced to gardens in the 17th century. It grows up to 15in (40cm) tall, with deeply divided leaves and bright blue flowers up to 2in (5cm) wide, with contrasting red stamens. The flowers are slightly fragrant and the seed pods are decorative. Selected forms have white or purple flowers. Hardy to 0°F (−18°C), US zones 7–10.

Love-in-a-mist *Nigella damascena* in Eccleston Square

Sweet peas trained on canes in the Wisley trials

Sweet peas trained on a fence

Sweet pea 'Blue Ice' and others

Sweet Pea

Lathyrus odoratus The wild form of the sweet pea is a vigorous, self-clinging hardy annual that grows to 7ft (2m) tall and produces intensely fragrant flowers, about 1½in (4cm) wide, in shades of pink and purple. It flowers for a long period over the summer and is good for cutting. Native to Italy, Sicily and Crete, it is hardy to 20°F (–6°C), US zones 9–10.

There is an enormous and ever-changing range of sweet pea cultivars in a great array of colours, and different seed merchants tend to name their own cultivars. Sweet peas are generally easy to grow and trained on tripods provide good filling for borders in the summer. Most are climbers and are excellent for growing up fences or through shrubs. Sweet peas are renowned for their scent, though not all varieties are strongly scented. Probably the most frequently grown group are the Spencer cultivars which are vigorous, scented, with large, slightly frilly flowers in most colours except yellow and are good for cutting.

PLANTING HELP Sweet peas may be sown from late winter to early spring at a depth of about ⅓in (1cm) and 2in (5cm) apart. In winter plant in a greenhouse and transfer to a cold frame after germination. The growing point should be pinched out when the first or second pair of leaves opens. Seedlings should be hardened off and planted out 9–12in (23–30cm) apart when the ground begins to warm up. Sweet peas need a sunny site and rich, well-drained soil with plenty of compost. Care should be taken that the soil does not dry out. Climbing varieties will need support in the form of a trellis, sticks or wire netting. In spring the seeds may be planted outside at a depth of 1in (2.5cm) in their flowering positions. Regular dead-heading will prolong the flowering season.

'Red Arrow'

'Suttons'

'Sarah'

'Felicity Kendal'

'Mrs Bernard
Jones'

'Blue Danube'

'Alan Titchmarsh'

'Esther Rantzen'

'Anniversary'

'Sally Unwin'

'Colin Unwin'

'Noel Sutton'

Specimens from Eccleston Square ⅓ life-size

Mixed colours of cornflowers in Eccleston Square

Sweet Sultan

Cornflowers

The following two plants used to be in the same genus and we have grouped them together under the cornflower heading for convenience. Modern farming methods mean that they are no longer found in cornfields in England. They make most attractive garden plants and a range of colours with larger, denser flowers is available.

PLANTING HELP   The annual species of cornflower are raised from seed sown where they are to flower, either in early autumn or early spring. Autumn-sown plants will grow taller and flower earlier, while successive sowings in spring will give a longer season. They will grow well in any well-drained, fairly fertile soil in full sun. Removing the dead flowers will prolong flowering.

Centaurea cyanus Cornflower   Native to most of Europe including the British Isles where it was once a common cornfield weed, and grown in gardens since the 16th century. It is an upright annual with narrow, grey green leaves and loose sprays of flowers 1–1½in (2.5–4cm) wide, which may be deep blue, white, pink or purplish red, borne over a long period from early summer to autumn. Taller varieties grow to about 3½ft (1m) and are good for cutting; more dwarf ones make bushy plants 1–1½ft (30–45cm) tall and provide colourful bedding or basket plants. Hardy to 0°F (–18°C), US zones 7–10.

Sweet Sultan *Amberboa moschata* (syn. *Centaurea moschata*)   Native to Turkey and the Caucasus, and has been grown in European gardens since the early 17th century. It is a bushy annual growing to 2ft (60cm) tall, with grey green foliage and sweetly scented, fringed flower heads, 2in (5cm) wide, from late spring to summer. Colours range from purple and pink to white and yellow. Hardy to 10°F (–12°C), US zones 8–10. As well as being a colourful bedding plant, Sweet Sultan is good for cutting.

Blue *Centaurea cyanus*

Centaurea cyanus 'Florence White'

Scabiosa stellata 'Paper Moon'

Scabious

Scabious are common perennials or annuals in dry meadows and fields in Europe. Their flat flower heads are followed by papery seed heads, which make the seeds blow further in the wind.

PLANTING HELP   Seed is sown in spring in pots or trays in a cold frame and planted out in early summer. Any well-drained soil in full sun.

Scabiosa atropurpurea   Native to S Europe, and has been grown in gardens since the early 17th century. The usual form has fragrant blackish purple or deep crimson flower heads, 2in (5cm) across, borne singly on long stems in summer above the coarsely toothed or lobed leaves. Other selections have pink or blue flowers. All grow 2–3ft (60–90cm) tall, and are hardy to 10°F (−12°C), US zones 8–10.

Scabiosa stellata   A small-flowered species from S Europe, grown mainly for its attractive, papery seed heads, which persist for many weeks. Stems to 12in (30cm); flower heads 1in (2.5cm) across. In **'Drumstick'** the fruiting heads turn brown; in **'Paper Moon'** they remain silvery for longer. Hardy to 10°F (−12°C), US zones 8–10.

Scabiosa stellata 'Drumstick'

Scabiosa atropurpurea 'Mixed Colours'

Mixed wallflowers in Eccleston Square

Erysimum cheiri 'Primrose Dame'

Wallflowers

Erysimum cheiri (syn. *Cheiranthus cheiri*)
Wallflowers are native to the eastern
Mediterranean region, where they grow on cliffs
and rocks, and can be found growing wild on
Roman and medieval walls throughout much of
Europe. Plants compact and rather shrub-like,
growing 12–24in (30–60cm) tall, with velvety
flowers, yellow in the wild, but varying from pink
and cream, through yellow and orange, to red and
brown in cultivated forms, in spring and early
summer. The flowers have a unique scent.
Wallflowers are one of the typical old-fashioned
flowers of spring, long used in cottage gardens or
in bedding schemes with bulbs, especially tulips
and forget-me-nots, all three flowering together.
Growing mixed colour forms together also makes
an attractive display. Hardy to about
0°F (–18°C), US zones 7–10.

PLANTING HELP
Wallflowers are perennials,
but are usually grown as
biennials. Sow seed outside
in seed beds in spring, then
in autumn transplant the
young plants to where
they are to flower during
the next spring. They
thrive in dry, well-
drained, preferably
limy soils and will not
tolerate waterlogged
conditions. Prefer a
sunny position.

Wallflowers

Snapdragons

Antirrhinum majus Cultivated snapdragons
come in a vast array of colours and are much more
compact than the 4ft (1.2m) wild form, which is
perennial and native to the Mediterranean region
and southwest Europe. The cultivars of
Antirrhinum majus shown here are generally grown
as half-hardy annuals. 'Double Madame Butterfly'
grows to 2ft (60cm), producing fully double
flowers about 1½in (4cm) long, in a wide range of
colours over a long period in summer. **'Apple
Blossom'** has more delicate flowers, white tinged
with pink, and grows to 3ft (90cm). The **'Liberty'**
varieties grow 2–2½ft (60–75cm), are more sturdy
and flower earlier. The **'Coronette'** series grow to
about 26in (65cm) and come in a wide variety of
colours. **'Candyman Mixed'** has flowers
attractively striped and stippled with red, on
strong plants to 15in (40cm) tall. Snapdragons are
hardy to 10°F (–12°C), US zones 8–10.

PLANTING HELP   Snapdragons do well in
most soil types, preferring a sunny site but will
tolerate a degree of shade. Seeds should be sown
inside in early spring, on the surface of the soil.
They should be left uncovered and the soil should
not be allowed to dry out. Germination usually
takes 10–14 days at 18–20°C (65–70°F). Seedlings
may be transplanted and grown in cooler
temperatures before being hardened off and
planted out when there is no longer any risk of
frost. To encourage continued flowering the flower
spikes should be removed as soon as they die. Rust
is often mentioned as a serious disease, but most
modern varieties are resistant to it.

Antirrhinum 'Apple Blossom'

Antirrhinum 'Liberty White'

Antirrhinum 'Coronette Pink'

Antirrhinum 'Candyman Mixed'

Large bed of *Antirrhinums* with scarlet *Tropaeolum speciosum* on the clipped yew behind, in Scotland

Sweet Alison

Lobularia maritima Native to open, rocky sites in the Mediterranean region and central Asia. The small plants, 3–6in (8–15cm) tall, bear slightly scented flowers from early summer to October. They are very good for edging and filling gaps in the rock garden or in wall crevices or paving stones. Cultivars are available in various colours, including cream, buff, white, pink and a pale crimson in **'Wonderland Red'**. Hardy to 10°F (−12°C), US zones 8–10.

PLANTING HELP   Sow seed outside where the plant is to flower from March to May. Alternatively, start them off indoors in February and plant out after hardening off, in late May. They like a well-drained soil and a position in full sun.

Candytuft

There are about 40 species of *Iberis* found in the wild, mostly in the Mediterranean region. The annual garden varieties are cultivars of *Iberis amara* or *Iberis umbellata*. They are useful, quick-growing plants for edging and borders and make good cut flowers. Dwarf varieties will grow happily in cracks in walls or paving stones. The flowers are often lightly scented and appear from June to September.
***Iberis amara* 'Giant Hyacinth-flowered'** bears dense spikes of white flowers, which, as the

Iberis 'Flash Mixed'

name would suggest, have a hyacinth-like appearance. This cultivar grows up to 15in (40cm) tall and is particularly good for cutting. Cultivars of *I. umbellata* have flatter groups of flowers and are available in a range of colours, including pinks, reds, lilac and white. **'Fairyland'** is a dwarf strain, up to 8in (20cm) tall. Hardy to 10°F (−12°C), US zones 8–10.

PLANTING HELP   Sow seed outside where the plant is to flower in March and September. Successive sowings will provide a continuous show of flowers. They grow best in a sunny position in well-drained soil.

Virginian Stock

Malcolmia maritima Native to the Mediterranean region and introduced to the rest of Europe in the early 18th century. Growing 8–16in (20–40cm) tall, it produces short racemes of sweetly scented, 4-petalled purple, red or white flowers ¾in (2cm) wide from spring to autumn, with narrow grey green leaves. Hardy to 10°F (−12°C), US zones 8–10. It is useful for edging.

PLANTING HELP   Seed is sown successionally where it is to flower, in late spring, to give a long season. Flowering starts about four weeks from sowing. It should have a well-drained soil in full sun and is generally trouble-free, although the leaves may be affected by downy mildew.

Stocks

Matthiola incana Gilliflower, Stock   Native to south and west Europe, it has been in cultivation since the early 18th century. It grows to 30in (75cm) with grey green leaves and very fragrant, four-petalled, purple flowers 1in (2.5cm) wide, borne in erect racemes from late spring to summer. Hardy to −10°F (−23°C), US zones 6–9.

Iberis 'Giant Hyacinth-flowered'

Iberis 'Fairyland'

Lobularia maritima
'Wonderland Red'

Virginian Stock

Matthiola incana Brompton Stocks

Many cultivars are much more compact and have single or double flowers that may be white, pink or purple. Those known as Ten-week Stocks are branched plants that grow to 18in (45cm) tall, flowering quickly from seed. **Brompton Stocks** are taller plants, grown as biennials. Both sorts are commonly sold in mixed colours.

Night-scented Stock *Matthiola longipetala*
Native to SW Asia and Greece, it was introduced to Europe in the early 19th century. An annual that grows to 12in (30cm) tall, this stock has narrow, grey green leaves and lilac pink flowers, ¾in (2cm) wide, strongly fragrant in the evening. Less showy than the other stocks, it is best sown among showier plants where its wonderful scent may be enjoyed in the evening.

PLANTING HELP   Seeds of the Ten-week and other annual stocks, including Night-scented Stock are sown in early spring. Biennials are sown in summer and overwintered under cloches.

Honesty

Lunaria annua   This biennial is native to much of Europe and is often found growing wild in recently disturbed ground. In late spring and summer it produces unscented four-petalled purple, dark pink or white flowers. These are followed by very attractive rounded, translucent seed pods, which are frequently dried and used in flower arrangements in the winter. The plants grow to 36in (90cm) tall. Several varieties are available, including 'Alba Variegata' with white flowers and leaves heavily variegated and blotched with white. Hardy to −10°F (−23°C), US zones 6–9, in well-drained soil.

PLANTING HELP   Sow seed outdoors in early summer. Transplant the young plants to the required flowering position in early autumn. Honesty needs moist but well-drained, fertile soil and will grow in sun or partial shade. It will self-seed if you do not pick the pods for decoration.

Honesty *Lunaria annua*

Night-scented Stock *Matthiola longipetala*

Chinese Forget-me-not *Cynoglossum amabile*

Foxglove 'Sutton's Apricot'

Cynoglossum

Chinese Forget-me-not *Cynoglossum amabile*
A bushy upright plant that grows 15–18in
(40–45cm) tall with grey green foliage and a mass
of forget-me-not-like flowers. Blue, pink and white
varieties are available. Native to eastern Asia.
Hardy to 0°F (–18°C), US zones 7–10. A useful
plant for adding colour to the early summer
border; it also attracts butterflies.

PLANTING HELP   Sow seeds indoors in mid-
spring in well-drained seed compost and keep at a
temperature of 70–75°F (20–24°C). The seedlings
can be transplanted when large enough to handle,
then hardened off and planted out in late spring.
Space the plants 12in (30cm) apart in well-drained
soil in full sun. They are susceptible to mildew.

Echium 'Blue Bedder'

Foxglove

Digitalis purpurea   Native to western Europe
and naturalized in North America and many other
countries, white foxgloves make an elegant
addition to both formal borders and more
informal 'cottage' gardens. Being shade-tolerant,
they are especially useful for growing under trees
or in other shaded areas. Their tall stems bear
many drooping, bell-shaped flowers from early to
midsummer. The blooms come in various colours
and are typically spotted inside. They are a great
favourite with bees and small insects. The leaves
are slightly hairy and greyish green in colour.
Note: all parts of the plant are poisonous if eaten
as they contain the heart drug digitalin.

Common or Purple Foxglove *Digitalis purpurea*
The familiar wild foxglove, this can grow to 6ft
(1.8m) tall. The flowers are purplish pink or white.
Hardy to –20°F (–29°C), US zones 5–9.

***Digitalis purpurea* 'Sutton's Apricot'**   This
has pale apricot pink flowers, slightly speckled
with pale green inside the mouth.

PLANTING HELP   Foxgloves should be
grown as hardy biennials, with seed sown in April
to produce leaves in the first year and flowers in
the second year. The seed can be sown *in situ* or in
containers in a cold frame. They prefer humus-
rich, well-drained soil and some shade, but will
grow under most conditions except extremes of
wet and dry.

Echium

Viper's Bugloss *Echium plantagineum*   An early summer-flowering plant, it bears short spikes of bell-shaped flowers and has bright green leaves covered with strong, whitish bristles. It is native to Europe. **'Blue Bedder'** has blooms of clear sky-blue opening from pink buds, while those of 'Dwarf Mixed' are purple, blue, pink and white. Both cultivars flower profusely and attract butterflies and bees. They make slightly unusual and attractive plants for a sunny border, growing happily in dry soil. They can also be grown in containers for the conservatory or a cool greenhouse. These cultivars of *E. plantagineum* grow up to 12in (30cm) tall and are hardy to −10°F (−23°C), US zones 6–9. Wild Viper's Bugloss *Echium vulgare* is a taller biennial, common on chalk downs or sand dunes.

PLANTING HELP   Sow seeds where they are to flower from March–May. Water regularly and thin seedlings to 6in (15cm) apart. Successive sowings will allow for continuous flowering from June–September and an autumn sowing should produce flowers in late spring. They need full sun and any well-drained, not too heavy soil; they grow very successfully on chalky soils.

Cerinthe

***Cerinthe major* 'Purpurascens'**
Native to southern Europe and introduced to gardens in the late 16th century. It is a hairless annual that grows to 2ft (60cm) tall, with nodding clusters of tubular yellow and purple flowers, 1¼in (3cm) long, in late spring and summer. Each flower arises from a conspicuous glaucous, bluish black bract. The oval

Cerinthe major 'Purpurascens'

leaves are an attractive blue green. Hardy to 10°F (−12°C), US zones 8–10.

PLANTING HELP   Cerinthe is raised from seeds sown *in situ* in early spring in any ordinary, fairly well-drained soil, in a sunny site. Alternatively, the seeds may be sown in autumn for earlier flowering and protected from excess cold and damp.

Common Foxglove *Digitalis purpurea* near Braemar, Aberdeenshire

Corn Marigold *Chrysanthemum segetum*

Chrysanthemums

Mostly native to the Mediterranean region, annual chrysanthemums are grown for their colourful daisy-like flowers. They are erect-stemmed plants and bloom for long periods throughout spring, summer and early autumn. They are easy to grow, and many make long-lasting cut flowers. Hardy to 20°F (−6°C), US zones 9–10 or lower and are usually grown as hardy annuals. Cultivars of three main species are the most popularly grown.

Chinese chrysanthemums are the familiar chrysanths of the florist and autumn garden; they have been called *Dendranthemum*, to distinguish them from other less shrubby *Chrysanthemum* species. The name *Dendranthemum* has now been rejected and the daisies shown on this page will get a new name.

PLANTING HELP   Sow seed outside where the plants are to flower in spring or early summer. In milder, frost-free areas an autumn sowing will produce early-flowering plants. They will grow in any well-drained, fairly fertile soil and like a sunny position.

Chrysanthemum carinatum (syn. *C. tricolor*) Native to Morocco, this annual bears large, single flowers which are generally white with rings of different colours and dark centres, from July to September. The plants grow 18–24in (45–60cm) tall. Several cultivars have been raised with flowers in a wide range of bright colours, including purple, red, yellow and white. **'Polar Star'** has white flowers with strong yellow rings on long, stiff stems. It is very good for cut flowers. **'Merry Mixture'** and 'Special Mixed' have flowers in many different colours.

Chrysanthemum coronarium   Native to southern Europe and the Mediterranean region, this plant produces yellow daisies, sometimes with rings of white or pink and dark centres from early spring to autumn. The cultivar **'Zebra'** has striking three-coloured flowers in strong shades of yellow and orange. *C. coronarium* grows up to 18in (45cm) tall. It is easy to grow in a group of mixed annuals, and in China the young leaves are eaten in salads, soups or stir-fries.

Corn Marigold *Chrysanthemum segetum*
A native wild flower, the corn marigold is a quick-growing plant with attractive bluish green leaves, and grows to 24in (60cm) tall. In summer it bears single, golden yellow daisies with large yellow or brown centres. It is a popular plant for wildflower gardens and will grow very successfully in even very chalky soils.

Chrysanthemum carinatum 'Polar Star'

Chrysanthemum carinatum 'Merry Mixture'

Chrysanthemum coronarium with fuchsias, golden hop and white *Micromeria*

Chrysanthemum coronarium 'Zebra'

Dianthus Lincolnshire Poacher

Dianthus chinensis 'Strawberry Parfait'

Dianthus chinensis 'Raspberry Parfait'

Dianthus 'Scarlet Charm'

Dianthus

Three groups of *Dianthus* are grown as annuals: annual Carnations, derived from *D. caryophyllus*, Sweet Williams and selections of *D. chinensis*.

PLANTING HELP   Seeds are sown in warmth in early spring and planted out in late spring. They like a well-drained, neutral or alkaline soil and a sunny position. Some are annuals, sown in spring, or biennials, sown in summer and planted out in autumn to flower the following year. Regular dead-heading will help to extend the flowering season. Pinks may be weakened by aphids and slugs may eat the foliage.

Dianthus caryophyllus   Native perhaps in the Mediterranean area and cultivated at least since the 16th century. Different varieties range from 10–30in (25–75cm) tall and have double flowers, often fragrant, about 2in (5cm) wide, in white, light yellow and a range of pink and red shades, as well as picotees. Hardy to 10°F (−12°C), US zones 8–10. Annual strains include the Lillipot Series that make compact plants about 9in (23cm) tall in a range of colours; and the Floristan Series which include some with picotee markings and grow to about 30in (75cm) tall.

Dianthus chinensis   Native to E Asia and introduced to Europe early in the 18th century. It is an annual that grows to 24in (60cm) tall, although most selections are more compact. The flowers are 1½in (4cm) wide, single or double, and may be white, pink or red with fringed petals and a

SWEET WILLIAM

A good bed of Sweet Williams for cutting at Drummond Castle

darker eye. Hardy to 0°F (−18°C), US zones 7–10.
'Raspberry Parfait' and **'Strawberry Parfait'**
are very compact plants to 8in (20cm) tall, with
single, deep pink flowers with a large crimson
central zone. The Heddewigii Group grows to
10in (25cm) or taller and has large double, very
fragrant flowers.

Sweet William *Dianthus barbatus* A short-lived
perennial often treated as a biennial that is native
to S Europe, but has long been a popular cottage
garden plant. Its strong stems, to about 2ft
(60cm), make it an easy plant for the garden, as it
needs no tying and staking, and produces large flat
heads of flowers throughout the summer. There
are several varieties available commercially,
including 'New Era' which is a true annual. Hardy
to −10°F (−23°C), US zones 6–10.

PLANTING HELP Sweet Williams are
usually grown from seed, sown indoors in late
spring, pricked out into trays and planted out into
the garden in the autumn. They like a sunny
position in well-drained but fertile soil. Ideal as
cut flowers and, indeed, it is important to pick
them regularly to prolong their flowering season.

Detail of Sweet William flowers

Dianthus caryophyllus 'Suffolk Summer'

45

Hibiscus moscheutos in a summer bedding scheme at Wisley

Hibiscus moscheutos 'Southern Belle'

Lavatera trimestris 'Mont Blanc'

Hibiscus

Swamp Rose Mallow *Hibiscus moscheutos*
Native to the eastern United States, this hardy
perennial, often grown as an annual, grows to 4ft
(1.2m) tall. In summer it produces huge, wide-
open flowers in white, pink or crimson, often with
a dark red zone at the base. Each flower is about
6in (15cm) wide. **'Southern Belle'** is a low-
growing selection with pink flowers. Hardy to
−20°F (−29°C), US zones 5–9. This handsome
plant is suitable for growing in containers and in a
conservatory.

PLANTING HELP *Hibiscus moscheutos* may
be planted *in situ* in late spring. It needs heat,
fertile soil, average rainfall and a sunny site. Pests
and diseases are not generally a problem.

Lavatera

Rose Mallow *Lavatera trimestris* This mallow is
of Mediterranean origin, particularly suitable for
planting in an herbaceous border and provides
good cut flowers. **'Pink Beauty'** grows to about
14in (35cm), and **'Mont Blanc'** to about 20in
(50cm). Petals overlapping at the base. Hardy to
20°F (−6°C), US zones 9–10.

PLANTING HELP Seeds may be planted
indoors in mid-spring at a depth of ⅛in (3mm) in
seed compost and kept at 70°F (20°C).
Germination takes 14–30 days. The transplanted
seedlings require good light and ventilation. When

Lavatera trimestris 'Pink Beauty'

all risk of frost has passed they may be hardened off and planted out in well-drained soil in a sunny position, about 24in (60cm) apart. Alternatively, seeds may be sown *in situ* in late spring. *Lavatera trimestris* is prone to rust.

Malope

Annual Mallow *Malope trifida*   Native to southern Spain, southern Portugal and North Africa, this hardy annual produces violet blue, white, pink or red flowers throughout the summer and grows to 36in (90cm) tall. The flowers are excellent for cutting, lasting well in water. They are similar to *Lavatera*, but are slightly smaller and have a gap between the base of each petal, forming a green star. Hardy to 20°F (−6°C), US zones 9–10.

PLANTING HELP   Seeds may be sown *in situ* from early to mid-spring. They should be planted ½in (1.5cm) deep in rows 12in (30cm) apart. Seeds require a temperature of about 55°F (13°C) to germinate. Although *Malope* will grow in most soils and partial shade, it prefers sun and a rich, well-drained soil. Dead-heading will prolong its flowering. This plant self-seeds freely.

Annual Mallow *Malope trifida*

Spider Flower *Cleome spinosa* 'Pink Queen' at Kew

Cleome

Spider Flower *Cleome spinosa* A tall summer-flowering annual with stems to 6ft (1.8m) in a good season. The scented flowers have long, spidery stamens which give the plant an exotic appearance. This half-hardy annual is suitable for filling in herbaceous or mixed borders and flowers in July–September. Most cultivars are in shades of purple, pink or white. Native to the tropics and subtropics, *Cleome* is hardy to 32°F (0°C), US zone 10. It is good for cutting.

PLANTING HELP Seeds may be planted in early spring under glass in sunlight, preferably in

loam-based potting compost. Seedlings should be hardened off and planted outdoors, 1½–2ft (45–60cm) apart, when the risk of frost has passed. *Cleome* needs a sunny site in fertile, well-drained soil. Plants should be watered freely during the growing season and dead-headed to prolong their flowering. *Cleome* may be prone to aphids and whiteflies.

Eustoma

Texan Bluebell, Prairie Gentian *Eustoma grandiflorum* (syn. *Eustoma russellianum, Lisanthius russellianus*) An erect annual or short-lived perennial that grows 1–3ft (30–90cm). In summer it produces large, bowl-shaped flowers, about 2½in (6cm) wide with broad overlapping petals in white, mauve, pink or purple. Native to the southern United States and Mexico and introduced to Europe in the early 19th century. Hardy to 20°F (−6°C), US zones 8–10. It is often grown indoors as a pot plant and is also grown commercially for cutting. Careful breeding has produced a wide range of colours and both tall, long-stemmed varieties and dwarf, bushy ones are available.

PLANTING HELP Seeds of this plant are normally sown in warmth in the early spring. *Eustoma grandiflorum* will grow in neutral to

Texas Bluebonnet *Lupinus texensis*

alkaline, well-drained soil and needs average rainfall. It may be planted outdoors in a sunny, sheltered position, but is more often grown as a pot plant for indoor decoration or in a greenhouse for cutting. Seeds will take 10–30 days to germinate. They should be left in the light with good ventilation. Seedlings should be planted out about 9in (23cm) apart and care should be taken not to over water them. Once in their flowering positions plants will need sticks for support. This plant is generally free from pests and diseases.

Lupins

Texas Bluebonnet *Lupinus texensis*
An annual species, the state flower of Texas, from where it originates. It bears many deep purple blue and white flowers on plants 10–15in (25–40cm) tall.

PLANTING HELP   The seedlings of annual lupins do not transplant well, so the seeds must be sown *in situ*. The seeds benefit from soaking in lukewarm water for one hour before sowing outdoors in spring, or in autumn in dry areas. Thin out the seedlings 12–18in (30–45cm) apart to allow room for plenty of flower spikes to develop. They prefer fairly fertile, well-drained soil and a position in full sun. Hardy to 10°F (–12°C), US zones 8–10.

Phlox

Annual Phlox *Phlox drummondii*   Native to Texas and New Mexico, this plant grows 8–24in (20–60cm) tall, and in summer and autumn produces large clusters of vivid, sometimes bicoloured flowers in a wide range of colours, including white, red, pink and purple, as well as intermediate tints. A wonderfully colourful summer bedding plant, this phlox is suitable for cutting and also makes a very effective container plant. Hardy to 20°F (–6°C), US zones 9–10.
Phlox drummondii **'Brilliant'**   This variety grows up to 20in (50cm) tall and bears flowers with strong rose pink centres fading to white at the edges of the petals.

PLANTING HELP   Sow seed indoors into good seed compost from late winter to early summer. They need warmth to germinate but once the seedlings are large enough to handle they can be transplanted and grown on in cooler conditions. Acclimatize gradually to outdoor conditions before planting out after all frosts have passed. The plants prefer a rich, well-drained soil and a position in full sun. The tips of the shoots should be pinched out to ensure bushy growth.

Cleome spinosa 'Cherry Queen'

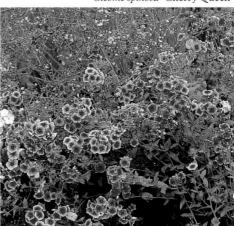

Phlox drummondii 'Brilliant'

Texan Bluebell *Eustoma grandiflorum*

49

Bartonia *Mentzelia lindleyi*

Bartonia

Blazing Star *Mentzelia lindleyi* (syn. *Bartonia aurea*)   Native to California, this plant has somewhat feathery, mid-green foliage and grows up to 18in (45cm) tall. It produces a succession of bright golden yellow flowers, strongly scented in the evening, from early summer to autumn. The flowers do not open on dull days, but this is more than compensated for by their spectacular appearance in the sun and their long flowering period. Hardy to 32°F (0°C), US zone 10.

PLANTING HELP   The seeds can be sown indoors in early spring, then hardened off gradually before planting out in late spring.

Nicandra physaloides, the large-flowered variety

Alternatively, they can be sown outdoors *in situ* from April. The seedlings should be kept about 9in (23cm) apart. They need a sheltered, sunny position in light, well-drained soil. They are easy to grow and generally free from pests and diseases.

Nicandra

Shoo Fly Plant, Apple of Peru *Nicandra physaloides*   Native to Peru, this plant, the only species in the genus, grows up to 36in (90cm) tall with large, wavy-toothed leaves. From July to September it produces pale violet blue, bell-shaped flowers with white throats, each about $1\frac{1}{2}$in (4cm) across. A large-flowered variety is also available, with flowers $2\frac{1}{2}$in (6cm) across, as is a deeper blue with dark buds **'Violacea'**. The flowers are short-lived and only open for a few hours each day. They are followed by fruits enclosed in Chinese lantern-like cases. Branches of these can be dried for use as winter decoration. Hardy to 32°F (–0°C), US zones 10. It makes an interesting border plant which, as its name suggests, is reputed to deter whitefly.

PLANTING HELP   Sow the seeds $\frac{1}{8}$in (3mm) deep in good seed compost from March to April, and maintain a temperature of 65–70°F (18–20°C) to facilitate germination. The seedlings can be transplanted when large enough to handle; acclimatize to cooler temperatures then plant out when all risk of frost has passed. They like a sunny position in well-drained soil and are generally free from pests and diseases.

Nolana humifusa 'Shooting Star'

Nolana paradoxa 'Blue Bird'

Nolana

A small genus of 18 species of tender annuals and perennials native to South America, from Chile to Peru. They make very good plants for hanging baskets or the edge of a sunny border. Hardy to 32°F (0°C), US zone 10.

Nolana paradoxa   Native to South America in Peru and Chile, and introduced to European gardens in the early 19th century. It is a low-growing perennial to 8in (20cm) tall, with rather sticky leaves and open trumpet-shaped flowers 2in (5cm) wide. The flowers are pale or deep blue with a white centre and yellow throat, or pure white.

Nolana paradoxa **'Blue Bird'**   A perennial usually grown as an annual, 6–8in (15–20cm) tall. Blue, bell-shaped flowers with wavy edges and creamy throats.

Nolana paradoxa **'Snowbird'**   The white flowers with yellow centres only open fully in bright sun.

Nolana humifusa **'Shooting Star'**   Long trailing purple stems bearing masses of bell-shaped flowers, greyish blue with purple veins. Wonderful for trailing from containers or hanging baskets. Hardy to 32°F (0°C), US zone 10.

PLANTING HELP   Sow seed *in situ* just below the surface in full sun. For early-flowering plants, sow seed in early spring at about 60°F (16°C), transplant to 3in (8cm) diameter pots and finally transplant into larger containers. Water freely and feed monthly during growth.

Nolana paradoxa 'Snowbird'

Nicandra physaloides 'Violacea'

Tropaeolum majus 'Salmon Baby'

Tropaeolum majus 'Empress of India'

Canary Creeper *Tropaeolum peregrinum*

Nasturtiums

Annual nasturtiums can provide reliable, easy-to-grow summer colour for all parts of the garden. The popular garden varieties are derived from *Tropaeolum majus*, a large and vigorous climber, native to Peru, which can be trained through trellises, used to cover pergolas or unsightly screens and fences, or allowed to creep along the ground. The smaller cultivars may be only semi-trailing or compact and are very good in window boxes, hanging baskets and other containers. The flowers and round, peltate leaves of nasturtiums are edible, having a pungent, peppery taste, and the flowers in particular, make a decorative, tangy addition to salads. The pickled buds and seeds of *T. majus* are a substitute for capers. Nasturtiums are susceptible to attack by black fly and the caterpillars of cabbage white butterflies. They are easily grown from seed, and once established will self-seed in mild winters. Nasturtiums are one of the first annuals to be killed by the autumn frosts, although they will overwinter in frost-free areas such as US zone 10.

***Tropaeolum majus* 'Alaska Mixed'** Grows to 8in (20cm) tall with flowers freely produced in several bright colours. They stand well above the distinctive foliage, which is light green speckled with white. Comes true to seed.

***Tropaeolum majus* 'Jewel of Africa'**
A climber that grows to 6ft (1.8m), this has flowers in various bright colours and, unusually for a climber, variegated green and cream foliage. Very effective in containers and hanging baskets.

***Tropaeolum majus* 'Empress of India'** This compact dwarf form grows to 9in (23cm) tall and has velvety flowers of deep crimson red above foliage of dark blue green edged with red.

***Tropaeolum majus* 'Salmon Baby'** This variety grows 9–12in (23–30cm) tall and has fringed flowers in an unusual shade of deep salmon pink. Forms a compact, bushy plant with flowers held above the foliage.

***Tropaeolum majus* 'Strawberries and Cream'** This variety grows 8–12in (20–30cm) tall and has semi-double flowers, pale yellow with a red spot at the base of each petal.

***Tropaeolum majus* 'Whirlybird Cherry'**
The Whirlybird nasturtiums grow to 12in (30cm) tall and have semi-double flowers without spurs which face upwards and are held well up above the low mounds of foliage. They are very free-flowering and are available in several colours, including the gold shade illustrated here.

PLANTING HELP Sow seeds outdoors from April to May, where they are to flower. They should be sown ¾in (2cm) deep 9–12in (23–30cm) apart, although seeds of some dwarf varieties need only be sown ¼in (0.5cm) deep. Seedlings may be thinned to 18in (45cm) apart, or 6in (15cm) for dwarf varieties. They need well-drained soil and a sunny position. *T. majus* and its cultivars flower best in relatively poor soils. If the soil is too rich, they will make masses of leaves at the expense of flowers. Water well on planting and again a week later, but only sparingly throughout the flowering season. For earlier flowering, the seeds can be sown indoors in early spring at 55°F (13°C). Seedlings should be hardened off before planting out after all risk of frost has passed. If growing a climbing variety through a shrub, do not use too many plants as they may swamp the host and damage its new growth.

Canary Creeper *Tropaeolum peregrinum*
A climber that grows to 6ft (1.8m) tall, with small, pale yellow, frilled flowers and pale green foliage, giving it a more delicate appearance than other climbing nasturtiums. It will grow in sun or shade and can do well on a north-facing wall, but requires a richer soil than other species and ample water while growing. It is ideal for quick cover or training through shrubs. Hardy to 32°F (0°C), US zone 10.

Tropaeolum majus 'Strawberries and Cream'

Tropaeolum majus 'Whirlybird Cherry'

Tropaeolum majus 'Alaska Mixed' in the potager at Ballymaloe Cookery School, Shanagarry

Himalayan Balsam *Impatiens glandulifera*

Impatiens Accent Series 'Coral'

Busy Lizzie

There are about 850 different wild species of *Impatiens*, native to tropical and warm-temperate regions, particularly mountainous areas of Asia and Africa. Some species have been grown as house plants for many years, but there are now numerous hybrids suitable for use as summer bedding. Planted in groups these will provide an effective display of colour, blending well with many other plants and flourishing in damp, shady areas. They are also suitable for all types of containers.

Impatiens walleriana Native to tropical East Africa, this has given rise to a wide range of named varieties with large flowers in various colours with some bicolours. They grow 6–10in (15–25in) tall. The **Accent Series** are compact plants available in many colours, some with star-shaped centres. Also pictured here are **'Dazzler Violet Star'** and a varigated scarlet hybrid.

New Guinea Group Derived from *Impatiens hawkeri* and other species from New Guinea, and valued for their brightly coloured or variegated leaves, as well as for their large flowers. These grow to 10in (25cm) tall. All these cultivars are easy to grow provided they have enough water and shade for part of the day. They can be grown in any zone, but will be killed by the first hard frosts in the autumn.

PLANTING HELP *Impatiens* cultivars can be raised from seed with careful handling, although young plants are always readily available at nurseries and garden centres at very reasonable prices. If using seed, it needs to be sown indoors in early spring and kept in warm, humid conditions until the seedlings are large enough to handle. At this stage they are prone to damping off. After hardening off, the young plants should be bedded out after all risk of frost has passed. For the hardy species, seed can be sown outside, where the plant is to flower. Impatiens will grow in any moist but well-drained soil and prefer partial shade.

Himalayan Balsam, Policeman's Helmet *Impatiens glandulifera* A much larger plant, growing up to 8ft (2.5m) tall. In late summer it produces hooded rose pink or purple flowers, followed by seed capsules which explode when touched, flinging the seeds away from the parent plant. Native to the Himalayas, it is now naturalized by rivers over much of Europe. Easily grown in a damp, shady place in the garden, and self-seeds very freely, so needs to be kept under control. The seedlings are easy to uproot when young. Hardy to 10°F (−12°C), US zones 8–10.

Impatiens 'Dazzler Violet Star'

Impatiens walleriana cultivars with tuberous begonias, purple *Ricinus* and *Nicotiana*

New Guinea *Impatiens* 'Ballet'

New Guinea *Impatiens* 'Illusion'

Impatiens, a mixed-colour, massed planting in Southsea, Hampshire

55

Variegated *Pelargonium* 'Mrs Parker'

White pelargoniums with purple verbena at Versailles

Pelargoniums

There is often confusion between geraniums and pelargoniums, some of the latter sometimes being referred to as geraniums. *Pelargonium* is a genus of evergreen or deciduous perennials and shrubs, mainly from South Africa, and hybridized in Europe since the early 18th century. *Geranium* is a genus of mostly hardy herbaceous perennials, found worldwide.

The pelargoniums used as annuals fall into the two main categories: Ivy-leaved pelargoniums, which are trailing plants with rather thick, glossy leaves that are ideal for pots and walls; and Zonal pelargoniums, whose leaves are softly velvety and often attractively marked with purple or brown and are generally used for bedding. Zonal pelargoniums can grow 12–18in (30-45cm) tall in a season. The single or double flowers, 1–2in (2.5–5cm) wide, borne in large clusters, may be white, pink, salmon, red or purple. They are perennials and are hardy to 32°F (0°C), US zone 10.

PLANTING HELP   Seeds of annual strains are sown in early spring under glass, at a temperature of about 60°F (15°C). They should be potted up prior to hardening off, and can be planted out in early summer, when there is no risk of frost. Cuttings can also be taken in the summer or early autumn, to overwinter for the following year, and many of the bedding varieties are cutting-raised anyway.

Pelargonium 'The Boar'

Variegated *Pelargonium* 'Caroline Schmidt'

Zonal pelargoniums with cannas in Hyde Park

Annual strain 'Sensation Mixed'

Zonal Pelargoniums   Often referred to as geraniums, these plants are extremely popular and are seen in gardens, greenhouses, window boxes, balconies and windowsills everywhere. They grow to 1–1½ft (30–45cm) tall in a season, bearing rounded leaves, often with a dark bronze zone from which their name is derived, and bear single or double flowers, 1–2in (2.5–5cm) wide, in shades of white, pink, salmon, red or purple, borne in large clusters.

'Caroline Schmidt'   A fine double-flowered variegated pelargonium, raised in Germany.

'Mrs Parker'   A pink sport of 'Caroline Schmidt', raised in 1880.

'The Boar'   An old trailing zonal with well-marked leaves and graceful flowers of an attractive pale orange. This is easily grown from cuttings planted out in spring and will thrive in poor soil and a warm position.

'Multibloom Lavender F1 Hybrid'   A seed-raised strain, also available in other colours, which will flower from seed the same summer.

'Sensation Mixed'   A seed-raised strain, which will flower from seed the same summer. Height to around 1ft (30cm).

'Multibloom Lavender F1 Hybrid'

Pelargonium 'Roller's Satinique'

Ivy-leaved pelargonium 'Decora Rose' at the Villa Torrigiani

Pots of 'Decora Rose' in Eccleston Square

Pelargonium 'Village Hill Oak' growing on Tresco, Isles of Scilly

Pelargoniums

These pelargonium are tough, free-flowering plants for poor soils and full sun. They have more trailing growth and smaller flowers than the zonals, but are free-flowering and often have scented leaves.

PLANTING HELP   All are easily raised from cuttings taken in summer, and may be planted out in spring to flower throughout the summer. They flower better if the soil has ample potash; too much nitrogen makes the plants produce leaves at the expense of the flowers. All are capable of surviving a few degrees of frost, 32°F (0°C), US zone 10, or a little less for a few days in dry soil.

Ivy-leaved Pelargoniums   These are trailing plants with rather thick, glossy leaves, derived from *Pelargonium peltatum*, first introduced into Holland in a consignment of plants sent by the Governor of Cape Province in 1700. This group is particularly good for hanging baskets, tubs and for clothing trelliswork. The leaves are 1–5in (2.5–12cm) across and somewhat resemble those of ivy. They bear clusters of single or double flowers 1½in (4cm) wide in shades of red, pink, mauve, purple or white.

***Pelargonium* 'Decora Rose'**   A plant with trailing growth to 1ft (30cm), bearing clusters of flowers, each 1¼in (3cm) wide, in summer. Hardy to 32°F (0°C), US zone 10. The Decora series are hybrids of ivy-leaved pelargoniums specially raised for summer use in window boxes and large pots. They have shortly trailing stems and come in a

PELARGONIUMS

Pelargonium 'Scarlet Unique' growing in an old garden on St Martins, Isles of Scilly

variety of shades from red to pink, lavender and salmon. 'Summer Showers' is a mixed, seed-raised strain.

Unique Pelargoniums   These are long-lived and I have seen large ancient patches in old gardens in as different places as the Isles of Scilly, Madeira, the coast of California and South Africa.
'Scarlet Unique'   An old hybrid, known since the 18th century, and now found throughout the world. It forms a spreading plant to 3ft (90cm).

Scented Pelargoniums   These shrubby evergreen perennials have rounded or lobed leaves 2–5in (5–12cm) across, which produce a characteristic scent when rubbed, bearing clusters of flowers in shades of white, pink, red, purple or peach, to 1¼in (3cm) across, throughout the summer. Many are old hybrids of *P. quercifolium* and other aromatic species crossed with hybrid groups such as the Regals or the Uniques.
'Roller's Satinique'   An attractive hybrid with bright pink, attractively marked flowers.
'Village Hill Oak'   This clone of *Pelargonium quercifolium* is one of the best species for growing outside in summer. Its small aromatic leaves are attractive and its flowers are freely produced when

it has a dry, sunny position. Plant spreading with stems to 3ft (90cm).
'Sweet Mimosa'   One of the toughest and most free-flowering of all pelargoniums, with pale pink flowers and scented leaves. Stems to 6ft (1.8m) if supported.

Pelargonium 'Sweet Mimosa'

Begonia tuberhybrida 'Non Stop Orange Improved', 'Non Stop Salmon' and 'Non Stop Yellow'

Begonia tuberhybrida 'Pin Up'   'Non Stop Pink'   'Fortune Peach Shades'

Begonias

These plants are native to moist tropical and subtropical regions of the world. Hundreds of species of *Begonia* are found in the wild, but those used as annual garden flowers are from two main groups. These are the Semperflorens fibrous-rooted begonias, and the Tuberhybrida begonias which have larger flowers and tuberous roots.

Begonia tuberhybrida Derived from a group of tuberous begonias native to the Andes, these spectacular plants can be upright or trailing, and bear large flowers, 3–6in (8–15cm) wide, from early summer to the first frosts. Planted in large groups they make striking bedding plants.

'Pin Up' is an award-winning hybrid, which can be raised from seed to flower the same year. The single flowers, 4–5in (10–12cm) wide, are white with a pink frilly edge. The **'Non Stop'** series comprises dwarf, early-flowering plants with double blooms in a range of colours such as orange, pink, salmon, scarlet, yellow and white. They reach 12in (30cm) tall and will flower right through to the autumn. Also pictured here are **'Fortune Peach Shades'** which, like many of the Tuberhybridas, is particularly recommended for containers. Begonias can be grown in any zone but their top growth will be killed by the first severe frosts.

Begonia semperflorens at Herrenhausen

Begonia semperflorens hybrids   Plants 6–18in (15–45cm) tall, with variety in both foliage and flower colour. The rounded, fleshy leaves may be green or bronze. The flowers, which can be single or double and ½–1in (1.5–2.5cm) wide, come in shades of red, pink and white, with some bicolours. A particular attraction of this group is that they flower equally well in sun or partial shade, making them useful bedding plants for shadowy areas.

PLANTING HELP   Both groups can be raised from seed, although the Semperflorens varieties are more usually grown from young plants purchased from a nursery and Tuberhybridas are grown from tubers. If growing from seed, start indoors in early spring and keep at a temperature of 60–70°F (15–20°C). Sow in a seed compost containing peat and sand, and only lightly cover the seed. Keep moist at all times, but not too wet. The seedlings should be hardened off gradually and planted out after all risk of frost has passed. Tubers should also be started off indoors in mid-spring and not planted out until the weather begins to warm up in June. However obtained, the young plants will grow best in humus-rich soil and with a cool, sheltered position in partial shade. Begonias are not drought-tolerant.

Mixed *Begonia semperflorens*

Begonia semperflorens

Salvia splendens 'Splendissima' at the Villa Pallavicino

Salvia coccinea 'Lady in Red'

Salvias

The salvias grown as summer annuals belong to a large and varied genus, which includes the aromatic sages, found in many temperate and tropical parts of the world. The annual members of this group and some perennial varieties grown as annuals, are generally valued for the strong, bright colours of their flowers. These are produced throughout the summer on erect spikes up to 2ft (60cm) tall. Salvias are extremely popular for mass bedding, especially when intense colour is wanted. The half-hardy varieties can be grown in any zone, but will be killed by the first frost.

PLANTING HELP   Sow seed indoors in warmth from March to April. They need moist but well-drained seed compost. Harden off the seedlings gradually and plant out after all risk of frost has passed, at which time it is also possible to sow seed outdoors where the plant is to flower. Salvias need a relatively rich, moist but well-drained soil. They all like a position in full sun.

Salvia splendens   The brilliant red of this plant is a familiar sight in parks and other public gardens. The species is native to Brazil and cultivars are available in many shades of pink, purple, white and especially red. Pictured here is the cultivar **'Splendissima'**, which grows 8–12in (20–30cm) tall, has very dense flower heads and tolerates both hot and humid or cool and wet conditions. Perennial but generally grown as a half-hardy annual.

Salvia coccinea **cultivars**   These have flowers in slightly softer colours which are more widely spaced on the stems, so they still provide good colour but with a less intense effect. **'Lady in Red'** has scarlet flowers and grows 12–15in (30–40cm) tall. Perennial, but grown as a half-hardy annual.

Salvia farinacea   Native to southern United States and Mexico. Several cultivars are available, with flowers in shades of blue, lavender and white. **'Strata'** has white stems and is very striking. Though actually perennial, they are grown as half-hardy annuals, and mix well with other border perennials as well as being good for cutting. They grow 14–24in (35–60cm) tall.

Salvia farinacea 'Strata'

Verbena
'Carousel'

Verbena

Most garden verbenas are cultivars of **Verbena ×
hybrida**. Although tender perennials, most are
generally grown as annuals. These may be upright
and bushy or spreading, mat-forming plants, with
flowers in a range of colours including red, pink,
purple, orange and white, reaching 10–18in
(25–45cm) tall. Verbenas can be grown in any zone
in summer, but will be killed by the first hard
frost. Several varieties are pictured here.

PLANTING HELP   Sow seed indoors in
warmth in early spring. Seedlings should be
hardened off gradually and planted out when the
weather begins to warm up. They need a
reasonably fertile, moist but well-drained soil and
like a position in full sun. Verbenas are susceptible
to mildew. Named varieties should be grown from
cuttings wintered away from frost.

Verbena 'Sissinghurst'

Verbena 'Pink Parfait'

Verbena 'Mauve Queen'

Verbena 'Stephen'

Schizanthus pinnatus 'Giant Hybrids' with cinerarias and stocks in a greenhouse

Schizanthus

Schizanthus pinnatus Poor Man's Orchid
Native to Chile and introduced to Europe in the
early 19th century. It is an erect annual that grows
to 24in (60cm) tall, with fern-like pale green
leaves. The clusters of exotic-looking flowers, 1½in
(4cm) wide, are produced from summer into
winter under glass. They are pink, red or white
with a yellow throat and are often spotted or
marked with deeper red or purple. Hardy to 32°F
(0°C), US zone 10. *Schizanthus* is usually grown in
a greenhouse or conservatory, but can also be used
for bedding outdoors in a warm, sheltered
position. **'Giant Hybrids'** will grow to 4ft (1.2m)
tall. In contrast, 'Star Parade' is a compact plant
that grows to 10in (25cm) tall, better suited to use
outdoors or in a small greenhouse.

PLANTING HELP   Seeds are sown in warmth
in early spring, or in late summer for winter
flowering under glass. Pinching out the tips to
encourage branching benefits the taller varieties.

Salpiglossis

Salpiglossis sinuata   An upright annual that
grows to 2ft (60cm) tall, with sticky stems and
foliage, native to Peru, Chile and Argentina and
introduced to Europe in the early 19th century.
The funnel-shaped flowers, about 2in (5cm) wide,
appear in summer and autumn; modern selections
and mixtures are available in a wide range of
colours including yellow, pink, salmon, purple,
blue purple and crimson, usually with beautiful
contrasting veining. Hardy to 32°F (0°C), US
zone 10.

PLANTING HELP   Seeds should be sown
under glass at a temperature of 60°F (15°C) or
higher, in the spring. The young plants should be
planted out only when there is no danger of frost.
They like a well-drained, fertile and fairly moist
soil in full sun, but should be sheltered from
strong winds. A few slender twigs pushed into the
ground will give unobtrusive support to the taller
varieties.

Salpiglossis 'Ingrid' with 'Royal Yellow' behind

Cuphea

Cuphea hyssopifolia A tender subshrub, native to Mexico, which can be grown as an annual. A spreading bushy plant that grows -to 24in (60cm) tall, with downy stems and narrow, dark green leaves. Small, 6-petalled pink, purple or white flowers are produced in summer and autumn. Hardy to 32°F (0°C), US zone 10.

PLANTING HELP Seeds are sown in early spring under glass, then hardened off before planting out when there is no risk of further frosts. In the garden it likes a sheltered, sunny situation, and does well in any moderately fertile soil.

Salpiglossis 'Carnival Mixed'

*Cuphea
hyssopifolia*

Salpiglossis 'Kew Blue'

Petunia 'Primetime Red Frost'

Petunia 'Peppermint Tart'

A petunia from the Ultra Star Series

Petunia 'Summer Sun'

Petunia 'Million Bells' in a hanging basket

Petunias

The garden petunias are of hybrid origin, their ancestors coming from South America. There are approximately 40 different wild species but many more cultivars have been bred for garden use. Petunias are very popular annuals, valued for their showy flowers produced over a long season, generally from late spring to early autumn. The main groups available are the Grandifloras, the Multifloras and the recently introduced Millifloras. All come in a variety of colours, mainly pinks, reds, yellows, violets or white. Some also have veined or striped petals, or contrasting edges or centres.

The Grandifloras have large flowers, up to 4in (10cm) wide. Some of these benefit from being grown in containers, as they are vulnerable to rain damage. The Multiflora group consists of bushier plants with a greater profusion of smaller flowers, up to 2in (5cm) wide. The Milliflora group has even smaller flowers. Both these latter groups make excellent bedding plants, giving a long show of colour over a large area. All petunias are much

Mixed petunias in a London area

used as plants for every type of container. They can be grown in any zone, but will be killed by the first frost.

'Million Bells'   A deep purple, small-flowered, trailing variety, perfect for hanging baskets.

Surfinia Series   Have medium-sized flowers and grow 9–16in (23–40cm) tall and are perennials, propagated by cuttings. These are particularly suitable for hanging baskets because of their vigorous trailing habit. Buy small plants in the spring.

Primetime Series   Multifloras growing up to 14in (35cm) tall and available in a large range of colours and multicolours.
'Summer Sun'   Another Multiflora; this is one of the best yellow petunias, growing up to 9in (23cm) tall.
'Peppermint Tart'   An example of a double-flowered petunia with large flowers.
Ultra Star Series   Have flowers with a narrow contrasting star from the middle.

PLANTING HELP   Sow seed indoors in early spring and keep at a temperature of 65–75°F (18–24°C). They need to go uncovered into a light seed compost, which should be kept moist, but not too wet. The seedlings should be hardened off gradually and planted out after all risk of frost has passed. Some hybrids are only available as young plants. These can be propagated from softwood cuttings in the summer, or bought from your local nursery. Protection from frost will be required for overwintering. Regular dead-heading will prolong the flowering period.

Petunia
'Surfinia Pink Vein'

Red Tobaccos, possibly 'Domino Red', with pelargoniums in Regents Park

Nicotiana 'Domino Lime'

Nicotiana 'Havana Appleblossom'

Nicotiana

Tobacco Plant or *Nicotiana* are half-hardy annuals which produce a succession of often colourful and sometimes sweetly scented flowers in summer. They originate from species native to South America. The most popular garden cultivars originate from *Nicotiana × sanderae*, a hybrid of *N. alata*, raised in 1903. It grows to 24in (60cm) tall, bearing clusters of red, white, pink or purple flowers 2in (5cm) across. Hardy to 0°F (−18°C), US zones 7–10. The flowers have a sweet scent, most noticeable in the evening; excellent for patio pots or window boxes, where this can be appreciated.

The **Domino** and **Havana Series** both produce dwarf plants, 10–12in (25–30cm) tall, which are heat- and shade-tolerant and are available in various shades of pink, red, green and white, with some bicolours. The **Domino Series** cultivars have more upward facing flowers. All have a sweet scent, most noticeable in the evening, so they are worth planting by a window where this can be appreciated. Tobacco plants are easily grown and can be used for colour in beds or containers. They can be grown in any zone, but will be killed by the first frost.

Nicotiana sylvestris with other tobaccos, *Cleome, Hosta plantaginea* and *Verbena* at Wave Hill, New York

Nicotiana 'Domino Picotee'

Nicotiana sylvestris, close-up of flowers

Nicotiana sylvestris A perennial with huge, soft leaves and stout stems to around 6ft (1.8m) that bear groups of long tubed, drooping white flowers. They are also scented in the evening. *N. sylvestris* makes a suitable border plant for both formal and cottage-type gardens. Hardy to 20°F (−6°C), US zones 9–10, if the roots are protected from freezing. **Note:** all parts of the tobacco plant are poisonous.

PLANTING HELP   Sow seed indoors in moist but not wet compost from late winter to early spring. They need warmth to germinate but once the seedling are large enough to handle they can be transplanted and grown on in cooler conditions. Gradually acclimatize to outdoor conditions before planting out after all threat of frost has passed. The plants prefer a rich, well-drained soil and a position in sun or partial shade.

Heliotropes at the Villa Pallavicino

Heliotropium arborescens 'Marine'

Calceolaria 'Yellow Speckle'

Heliotrope

Heliotropium arborescens Cherry Pie   Native to Peru and introduced to Europe in the mid-18th century. A tender sub-shrub that can grow to 6ft (1.8m) tall, it is generally grown as an annual and then forms a bushy plant 12–24in (30–60m) tall. Dense sprays of small, sweetly scented, violet purple flowers are borne above the wrinkled, ovate, dark green leaves, for a long period in summer. Hardy to 32°F (0°C), US zone 10. Numerous selections are available, mostly more compact, with flowers ranging from deep purple, to violet blue and white. **'Marine'** grows to 18in (45cm) and has rich violet blue flowers.

PLANTING HELP   Cherry Pie is normally treated as an annual or half-hardy perennial, planted outside, either in the border or in a pot, once the danger of frost has passed. It is also very effective as a plant for a cool conservatory, where its scent can be appreciated at close quarters. Cherry Pie can be grown from seed sown indoors in early spring or from small plants obtained from a nursery. It does best in good moist, but well-drained soil in sun or partial shade, and should be

Calceolaria 'Sunset Red'

Mimulus 'Magnifique'

watered freely during the growing season. Large plants grown as standard specimens outside can be dug up, brought into the greenhouse and potted up for the winter.

Slipper Flower

Calceolaria is a genus of 300 species, native to Central and South America, mainly Chile, Peru and Mexico. From June to October they bear brightly coloured flowers which, as the common name would suggest, are slipper-shaped. Although some species have long been grown for spring flowering in the greenhouse, modern shrubby hybrids are now used for bedding. They are now available in bright shades of red, orange or yellow, some with contrasting speckles. Most varieties grow up to 12in (30cm) tall. There are dwarf hybrids available, but these are usually only suitable for growing as greenhouse annuals. The outdoor calceolarias can be grown in any zone, but will be killed by the first frost.

PLANTING HELP   The seeds are extremely small and require careful handling. Sow indoors in early spring and keep at a temperature of 65–75°F (18–24°C). They need to go uncovered into a light seed compost, which should always be kept moist, but not too wet. The seedlings should be hardened off gradually and planted out after all risk of frost has passed. They like a light, fairly rich soil and a position in full sun or partial shade.

Mimulus

Monkey Flower is native to North and South America, usually growing in damp, boggy areas. It was introduced to Europe in the 18th century. Several species of *Mimulus* are cultivated and some have escaped onto streambanks in Europe. The hybrids grown as summer bedding are actually tender perennials, but are usually treated

as half-hardy annuals. Over a long period in summer and autumn they produce open-mouthed, trumpet-shaped flowers. They are available in many shades of red, orange and yellow, often with contrasting speckles. Pictured here is **'Magnifique'** which grows up to 12in (30cm) tall and has pale yellow flowers spotted with red. Also shown are several members of the **Magic Series**, smaller cultivars, 6–8in (15–20cm) tall, which have flowers in several bright and pastel shades. Mimulus are water-loving and shade-tolerant, so can be used for bedding in damp, shadowed areas, and are very good for window boxes and containers on north-facing walls. They can be grown in any zone but will be killed by hard frost.

PLANTING HELP   Sow seed indoors in mid-spring. Seedlings should be hardened off gradually and can be planted out as soon as the last frost has passed. They must have moist, humus-rich soil which is not allowed to dry out. These plants will tolerate full sun, but grow happily in full or partial shade.

Mimulus 'Magic Wine'

Climbing Snapdragon *Lophospermum erubescens*

Morning Glory

These twining climbers bear numerous colourful, trumpet-shaped flowers from midsummer to autumn. *Ipomoea* make good container plants for a conservatory or greenhouse, and in sheltered positions, provide attractive cover for sunny walls and fences. They can also be safely grown through other plants to add colour contrast or to prolong the colour interest in an earlier-flowering shrub or small tree.

PLANTING HELP   Seeds should be sown individually in pots in the early spring after soaking overnight or notching. A temperature of around 70°F (25°C) is required for germination, but the seedlings should be kept cooler to prevent too rapid growth. They need careful acclimatization to outdoor temperatures before planting out, which should be done when summer has arrived. Morning glories need well-drained, leafy soil and a warm, sunny, sheltered position. Regular dead-heading will prolong flowering. If grown in a conservatory the plants need frequent spraying to keep red spider mites at bay. **Note:** the seeds of *Ipomoea* are **very** poisonous.

Ipomoea purpurea   A perennial climber that grows to 16ft (4.5m) tall, bearing deep blue or purple flowers, about 3in (8cm) long. Not hardy below 32°F (0°C), US zone 10. Thought to be native to Mexico, this morning glory is a popular climber in temperate and warmer regions.

Ipomoea tricolor **'Heavenly Blue'**   A climber that grows to 12ft (3.5m) tall with bright sky blue flowers, 3in (8cm) long. Not hardy below 32°F (0°C), US zone 10. Native to Mexico and Central America, it is a beautiful climber for a sunny wall, equally suitable for a conservatory.

Climbing Snapdragon

Lophospermum erubescens (syn. *Asarina erubescens*)   An attractive, quick-growing, twining perennial that can be grown as an annual. It grows to 6ft (1.8m) and bears deep pink snapdragons, 2in (7cm) long, from midsummer to the first frosts. Well-suited to containers, indoors or out. Not hardy below 32°F (0°C), US zone 10. Native to southern Mexico, where it is perennial.

Ipomoea tricolor 'Heavenly Blue'

Morning Glory *Ipomoea purpurea*

PLANTING HELP   Sow seeds indoors from
late winter to spring, later if the plants are for a
greenhouse or conservatory. Seedlings should be
planted out after all risk of frost has passed, in a
warm, sunny, sheltered position. They like neutral
or alkaline, well-drained soil and a cool root run.
Water regularly in dry weather.

Purple Bell Vine

Rhodochiton atrosanguineum   This unusual and
elegant climber grows to 10ft (3m) tall and has
heart-shaped leaves with twining stalks. From
midsummer to autumn it bears pendulous,
tubular, almost black flowers, each about 2½in
(4cm) long, with white stamens from a maroon or
reddish purple bell-like calyx. Native to Mexico, it
is hardy to 20°F (−6°C), US zones 9–10.

PLANTING HELP   Seedlings raised indoors
in early spring can be bedded out in late spring
after all risk of frost has passed, or grown in pots in
a cool, shady greenhouse or conservatory. Support
should be provided to allow it to climb tall enough
to show off the pendent flowers. It needs a moist
but well-drained, fairly fertile soil and a cool,
partially sunny position, and will survive the
winter in mild areas.

Rhodochiton atrosanguineum Purple Bell Vine

Senecio

Senecio cineraria   Native to the
Mediterranean region, these sub-shrubs are
suitable for bedding or for use in containers. The
hairy, silvery grey leaves grow to about 6in (15cm)
long and the rather insignificant yellow flowers are
borne in summer. They are good for planting on
the coast where they tolerate salt wind and are less
subject to frost. Both cultivars shown here,
Senecio cineraria **'Cirrus'** and **'Silver Dust'**,
grow to about 12in (30cm) tall. Hardy to 20°F
(–6°C), US zones 9–10.

PLANTING HELP   *Senecio cineraria* will grow
from seed or cuttings in any well-drained soil and
a sunny position. It is prone to aphids, rust, red
spider mite and whitefly. **Note:** all parts of this
plant are poisonous.

Brassica

Ornamental Cabbage *Brassica oleracea*   These
cabbages are grown for their foliage. They provide
interest in autumn or winter bedding schemes and
are suitable for containers. Their somewhat
artificial-looking leaves may be red, pink or white,
their brightness depending on the degree of cold;
they are brighter when the night temperature falls
below 50°F (10°C). Hardy to 0°F (–18°C),
US zones 7–10.

PLANTING HELP   Seeds may be sown *in situ*
in spring, or under glass if planted in early spring.
This plant prefers a sunny site and well-drained,
fertile soil, preferably rich in lime.

Capsicum

Chilli Pepper Paprika *Capsicum annuum*   Native
to Mexico and Central America, most varieties of
Capsicum are grown as vegetables, and those with
bright red, shiny fruits, such as Red Chilli, can be
very decorative. A distinct group with cherry-like
fruits have been raised for winter decoration.
Small, starry white flowers in summer are followed
by the round, red, shiny fruit.

PLANTING HELP   Seed may be sown in late
winter at a temperature of 70°F (21°C). During
hot weather plants may be transferred to a
sheltered site outside. If grown in a greenhouse
good air circulation should be maintained to avoid
mould in damp autumn weather.

Tanacetum

Tanacetum ptarmiciflorum (syn. *Pyrethrum
ptarmiciflorum*)   Native to the Canary Islands,
this half-hardy annual is a useful bedding plant,
suitable for the edge of a border. It grows to about
24in (60cm) tall and 16in (40cm) wide. The hairy
silver leaves, for which it is grown, are about 4in
(10cm) long, and its white and yellow daisy-like
flowers are borne in late summer. Hardy to 20°F
(–6°C), US zones 9–10. **'Silver Feather'** is more
compact than the wild plant.

PLANTING HELP   Seeds should be sown in
late winter or early spring, at 53°F (12°C). It
should be planted out in early summer in a sunny
position, in well-drained soil. It may be susceptible
to leaf miners.

Senecio cineraria 'Cirrus'

Senecio cineraria 'Silver Dust' planted with *Lobelia* and *Ageratum* in
the Moon garden at Colgrave Seeds

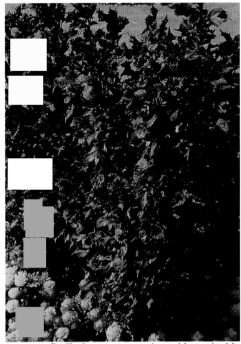
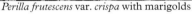

Perilla frutescens var. *crispa* with marigolds

Ornamental cabbages and red lettuces

Perilla

Perilla frutescens Native to eastern Asia and introduced to Europe in the mid-18th century. An erect, bushy annual that grows up to 3½ft (1m) tall, it has insignificant, tubular white flowers, borne in spikes in summer. However, it is grown for its attractive and pleasantly aromatic foliage rather than the flowers. The broadly ovate leaves are up to 5in (12cm) long, deep bronze purple with incised and crisped margins in **var. crispa** (syn. var. *nankinensis*). Hardy to 10°F (−12°C), US zones 8–10. It is a striking foliage plant and provides an effective contrast to brightly coloured flowers.

PLANTING HELP

Seeds are sown in warmth in spring and planted out in late spring. It should have a position in partial or full sun and a fertile, fairly moist soil.

Capsicum annuum 'Aladin'

Perilla frutescens
var. *crispa*

Tanacetum ptarmiciflorum

Love-lies-bleeding *Amaranthus caudatus*

Amaranthus

The genus *Amaranthus*, including the popular Love-lies-bleeding, is native to tropical regions and some species were introduced to Europe by the 16th century. They are annuals, some prostrate, others upright in habit, with large leaves and tiny flowers packed into dense tassels or spikes. Hardy to 32°F (0°C), US zone 10.

PLANTING HELP   Seed of the various *Amaranthus* species is sown in a warm greenhouse at about 68°F (20°C) in spring. Often grown for greenhouse decoration, they may be planted out for summer bedding in late May or early June, giving a colourful and exotic effect. They prefer fertile, moisture-retentive soil in sun or partial shade, and should have plenty of water during hot and dry weather.

Love-lies-bleeding *Amaranthus caudatus*
This has long drooping crimson tassels and grows to 2ft (60cm) tall.
***Amaranthus caudatus* 'Viridis'** (syn. 'Green Tails')   This has long green tassels which trail on the ground. The stems reach around 3ft (1m) tall.

Celosia

Celosia argentea   Native to tropical parts of Asia, Africa and the Americas, this plant was introduced to Europe in the mid-16th century. An erect perennial that grows to 2ft (60cm) tall, it is usually treated as an annual. Over a long period in summer, it produces upright silvery white or pink flower heads. However, the many cultivated selections are far more showy, with large, erect feathery flower heads, which may be yellow, as in **'Golden Triumph'**, orange as in **'Apricot Brandy'**, or pink or red. In the **Olympia Series**, one of the Cristata group, the flower heads are flat

Amaranthus caudatus 'Viridis'

Celosia argentea 'Golden Triumph'

and crested. Most are more compact and several grow to only 8in (20cm) tall. Hardy to 32°F (0°C), US zone 10; it is also grown for greenhouse decoration.

PLANTING HELP   Seeds of this plant should be sown in warmth in early spring, preferably in a propagating case or greenhouse kept at 64°F (18°C). The seedlings should be hardened off before planting out when all danger of frost has passed, in a fertile, moist soil in full sun. This plant is rather susceptible to root rot and fungal leaf spots.

Castor Oil Plant

Ricinus communis   Native of North Africa and the Middle East, this plant is usually grown as a half-hardy annual, reaching about 5ft (1.5m) tall. The Castor Oil Plant is grown for its spectacular foliage, which in some varieties may be a rich red or purple. 'Carmencita' is a tall variety with bronze foliage; **'Impala'** has purple leaves on a shorter plant, usually reaching 4ft (1.2m). Hardy to 32°F (0°C), US zone 10. **Note:** all parts of the Castor Oil Plant are **deadly poisonous**, particularly the seeds. Touching the foliage may cause severe rashes.

PLANTING HELP   Seeds should be soaked for 24 hours before sowing in pots at 70°F (21°C). Seedlings should then be repotted and placed in a reduced temperature of about 55°F (13°C). They may be planted out when all risk of frost has passed in late spring. *Ricinus communis* needs a rich, fertile, well-drained soil and a sunny site. If grown under glass it needs a light position and well-fertilized, loam-based potting compost. In hot and dry conditions red spider mites may prove to be a problem. Care should be taken not to over-water in winter.

Castor Oil Plant *Ricinus communis* 'Impala'

Castor Oil Plant *Ricinus communis*, young fruit

Celosia 'Apricot Brandy'

Celosia argentea Olympia Series

Aster 'Giant Single'

Aster 'Duchess Mixed'

Aster 'Craw Krallenaster'

Chinese Aster

Callistephus chinensis There are numerous varieties of these annual asters available, all derived from one species native to China. They are some of the best late-flowering annuals, blooming well into the autumn. The daisy- or chrysanthemum-like flowers may be single, semi-double or double, and come in a wide range of colours from strong reds and purples to pale yellows and whites. Dwarf varieties grow 6–12in (15–30cm) tall, while the taller varieties can reach up to 2ft (60cm).

Examples of chrysanthemum-flowered varieties are the tall **Duchess** group, with attractive incurved petals. The **'Craw Krallenaster'** mixture have quilled petals and come in some softer colour shades. **'Giant Single'** is a tall erect variety, suitable for cutting. Asters can be grown in containers as well as in borders, and the taller varieties make very good, long-lasting cut flowers. They can be grown in any zone but will be killed by the first hard frost.

PLANTING HELP   Sow seed indoors in warmth in early spring. Harden off the seedlings gradually and plant out after all risk of frost has passed. In milder areas the seed can be sown outside where the plant is to flower, from mid-April onwards. They like neutral to alkaline, moist, well-drained soil and a position in full sun. Asters are prone to aster wilt, so should be grown in a different position every year. The taller varieties will need staking. Regular dead-heading will prolong the flowering period.

Ageratum possibly 'Blue Horizon' at Arley Hall

Ageratum

Ageratum houstonianum Floss-flower Native to Mexico and introduced to gardens in Europe in the early 19th century. It is an erect annual that grows to 2ft (60cm) tall, with clusters of fluffy blue, mauve, pink or white flower heads, held above rounded leaves, from midsummer to late autumn. Hardy to 10°F (−12°C), US zones 8–10. It is a valuable bedding plant with a long flowering season. Selective breeding has resulted in a wide range of varieties differing in habit, size and flower colour, of which bushy dwarf ones are most popular. **'Southern Cross'** has two-tone blue and white flowers and grows to 12in (30cm) tall. **'Blue Horizon'** has tall stems to 18in (45cm), and rain-tolerant flowers.

PLANTING HELP Seeds are sown in warmth in early spring and planted out in late spring. It likes fertile, fairly moist soil and a sunny, sheltered position and should be watered freely in hot, dry weather to maintain flower production. Generally trouble-free but liable to rot at the roots.

Ageratum 'Blue Champion'

Ageratum 'Southern Cross'

Everlasting flowers *Helichrysum bracteatum* in San Francisco

Acroclinium

Acroclinium roseum (syn. *Helipterum roseum, Rhodanthe chlorocephala* subsp. *rosea*)   Native to Australia, this plant bears colourful, daisy-like 'everlasting' flowers from July to September. The flowers come in white or a range of shades of pink with yellow or black centres, held on erect stems 12–18in (30–45cm) tall. They have straw-like petals and can be cut and dried for use in flower arrangements. Hardy to 32°F (0°C), US zone 10.

PLANTING HELP   Seed should be sown indoors in early spring and the seedlings planted out after all risk of frost has passed. They like a position in full sun and flourish in poor, dry soil. For drying, the flowers should be cut just before they are fully open and hung upside down in a dark, dry and cool place.

Everlasting Flower

Helichrysum bracteatum (syn. *Bracteantha bracteata*)   This brightly coloured plant, originally from Australia, is popularly grown for cutting and drying, but also makes an attractive border filler or container plant. Some varieties are perennial, but a number of annual strains have been developed, especially for use as everlastings. From early summer to autumn it bears 'everlasting' flowers which look like double daisies with shiny, papery petals. Many cultivars are now available in a wide

range of colours, including yellows, reds, pinks, oranges and white, some with double flower heads. They grow from 1–5ft (30–150cm) and the taller varieties may need staking. Hardy to 32°F (0°C), US zone 10.

PLANTING HELP   Sow seed indoors in early spring. They need good seed compost and a temperature of 70–75°F (20–24°C). The seedlings should be hardened off and planted out after all risk of frost has passed. They like a well-drained soil and a position in full sun. For drying, the flowers should be cut as soon as they begin to open and hung upside down in a dark, dry and cool place.

Everlasting flowers
Helichrysum bracteatum

Yellow Sea Lavender *Limonium sinuatum,* at the University Botanic Garden, Cambridge

Statice

Sea Lavender

Limonium sinuatum
(syn. *Statice sinuata*)
A colourful annual
with flat-topped sprays
of flowers suitable for
drying. Native to the
Mediterranean region
where it grows in dry
sandy places. For a
long period in
summer the stiff
winged stems, to 3ft
(90cm) tall, produce small
white flowers within a
brightly coloured calyx. The
calyxes retain their colour when
dried and the plant is mostly
grown for winter flower
arrangements. Hardy to 10°F
(–12°C), US zones 8–10. Many
varieties are available with flowers in a
range of colours.

Limonium sinuatum 'Sunset'

PLANTING HELP   Sow seed indoors
in early spring. The seedlings should be
hardened off and planted out when the
weather begins to warm up. They like a light, well-
drained soil and a position in full sun. For drying,
the flowers should be cut as soon as they begin to
open, tied in bunches and hung upside down in a
dark, dry and cool place.

Limonium sinuatum 'Heavenly Blue'

Acroclinium roseum

Coreopsis grandiflora 'Early Sunrise'

Coreopsis grandiflora 'Sunray'

Coreopsis tinctoria 'Standard Tall Mixture'

Coreopsis basalis 'Golden Crown'

Coreopsis

Annuals and perennials native to North and Central America, which bear many large, daisy-like flowers for a long period over the summer. The flowers come in shades of yellow, orange and dark red. Some of the perennial species are short-lived and are better grown as annuals, flowering from seed in the first year. With both long-stemmed and dwarf varieties available, they make excellent border plants and are good for cutting. Hardy to 10°F (−12°C), US zones 8–10.

PLANTING HELP   Sow seeds of the annual varieties outside where they are to flower, from mid-spring to early summer. Thin seedlings 9–12in (23–30cm) apart. Perennial varities can be raised in trays or seedbeds from seed sown outside

Coreopsis grandiflora 'Badengold'

in March or indoors in late winter. *Coreopsis* will grow in any well-drained garden soil and like a sunny position, although the perennial varieties will tolerate partial shade. Tall varieties may need staking. Regular dead-heading will prolong the flowering period.

***Coreopsis basalis* 'Golden Crown'** (syn. *C. drummondii*)   An annual native to Texas, this plant grows up to 2ft (60cm) tall and bears golden yellow flowers, 3in (8cm), with dark red centres.

Coreopsis grandiflora   The perennial varieties of *Coreopsis grandiflora* which produce solitary, sometimes semi-double or double, flower heads on slender stems, 18–36in (45–90cm) tall. **'Badengold'** is a tall single-flowered cultivar. **'Early Sunrise'** has semi-double flowers and **'Sunray'** is a double-flowered example. 'Mayfield Giant' and 'Early Sunrise' are also sold as seed, and can be grown as annuals.

***Coreopsis tinctoria* 'Standard Tall Mixture'** (syn. *Calliopsis tinctoria*)   This annual has yellow flowers with striking, dark red centres and grows up to 3ft (90cm) tall.

Coreopsis grandiflora

Helianthus annuus 'Moonwalker'

Helianthus annuus 'Big Smile'

Helianthus annuus 'Velvet Queen'

Sunflowers

Helianthus annuus was introduced into cultivation from its native South America in the 16th century. In summer it produces the well-known huge, bright yellow flowers on stems up to 10ft (3m) or more, tall. Each flower is about 1ft (30cm) across with a large brown or reddish centre. Sunflowers make good cut flowers and the fruiting head may be used for dried flower decoration or left for the birds to take the seeds. Hardy to 32°F (0°C), US zone 10. It is now available in many selected forms which vary greatly in height, size and number and colour of flowers, making it possible to find a suitable sunflower for most areas of a sunny border.

PLANTING HELP   Seeds may be sown outdoors *in situ* from mid-spring to early summer. They should be planted ½in (1.5cm) deep in well-worked garden soil. The seedlings should be thinned 12–18in (30–45cm) apart. They prefer well-drained soil and a sunny position but will grow in most garden soils and tolerate partial shade. For earlier flowering they can be started off indoors in early spring at a temperature of 70°F (20°C). Tall plants will need some support. Sunflowers are generally free from pests and diseases.

***Helianthus annuus* 'Big Smile'**   An easily grown dwarf variety that grows 12–18in (30–45cm) tall and is suitable for containers as well as beds and borders. The golden yellow flower heads are up to 4in (10cm) across.

SUNFLOWERS

Helianthus annuus 'Italian White'
This variety grows up to 4ft (1.2m) tall, and has
striking cream coloured 4in (10cm) flowers with
black centres.

Helianthus annuus 'Moonwalker'   A bushy,
free-branching form, growing 48–60in
(125–180cm) tall. Each stem bears several large,
lemon yellow flowers, with dark chocolate centres.

Helianthus annuus 'Teddy Bear'   This is a
very dwarf variety, only reaching 2ft (60 cm) tall,
with large and spectacular, very double, golden
yellow flowers, up to 6in (15cm).

Helianthus annuus 'Titan'   A giant sunflower
in all senses of the word, this can grow up to 12ft
(3.5m) tall, with very large golden yellow flower
heads, up to 2ft (60cm) across.

Helianthus annuus 'Russian Giant'   A typical
tall variety which grows 8–10ft (2.5–3m) tall and
with 10in (25cm) flower heads.

Helianthus annuus 'Velvet Queen'   This free-
flowering form grows up to 5ft (1.5m) tall, and has
flowers of a wonderful deep velvety red with much
darker centres.

Helianthus annuus 'Titan'

Helianthus annuus 'Teddy Bear'

Helianthus annuus 'Russian Giant'

Helianthus annuus 'Italian White'

Rudbeckia

A small genus native to North America, *Rudbeckia* or Coneflower was introduced to Europe in the late 18th century. There are many hybrid strains, now mostly easily grown annuals for sunny borders or beds. From summer to autumn they produce large daisy-like flowers in yellow, orange or bronze red with dark, cone-like centres, a single flower to each stem. They are excellent for cutting.

PLANTING HELP   Sow seed indoors in moist compost in late winter or early spring. Harden off seedlings gradually before planting out in a sunny position in moist but well-drained soil. Rudbeckias are often attacked by slugs. Taller varieties may need staking.

Rudbeckia amplexicaulis (syn. *Dracopis amplexicaulis*)   Native from Missouri and Oklahoma, south to Louisiana and Texas, in wet places, this species grows up to 3ft (90cm) tall, and in summer produces yellow flowers with black

centres, 2–3in (5–8cm) wide. The bluish green foliage can suffer from a white mildew in dry soils. Hardy to −10°F (−12°C), US zones 8–10.

Black-eyed Susan *Rudbeckia hirta*   Native to North America from Ontario to Manitoba, south to Florida and Texas, growing 2–3ft (60–90cm) tall. It bears pale to golden yellow flowers with dark brown centre cones, each 3in (8cm) wide. The flowering period lasts from early summer well into the autumn. Hardy to 20°F (−29°C), US zones 5–9.

***Rudbeckia hirta* 'Goldilocks'**   This form has long-lasting, golden yellow, double or semi-double flowers and reaches up to 24in (60cm) tall. Hardy to 10°F (−12°C), US zones 8–10.

***Rudbeckia hirta* 'Becky Mixed'**   A dwarf mxture that grows to 10in (25cm) tall and is useful for the front of a border or in containers. The flowers, produced from early summer up to the first frost, are very large, up to 6in (15cm) across,

Bidens ferulifolia 'Golden Goddess'

Rudbeckia amplexicaulis

Rudbeckia hirta 'Gloriosa Mixed'

Rudbeckia hirta 'Goldilocks'

with lemon and golden yellow petals and contrasting darker centres. Hardy to 10°F (−12°C), US zones 8–10.

***Rudbeckia hirta* 'Gloriosa Mixed'** A tall variety, up to 36in (90cm) tall, with very large flower heads, some reaching 7in (18cm) across, in autumnal shades. Hardy to 10°F (−12°C), US zones 8–10.

***Rudbeckia hirta* 'Rustic Dwarfs'** In summer this variety produces golden yellow, orange, bronze or mahogany flowers, sometimes bicoloured, with black cones. Each flower is about 5in (12cm) across on stems up to 2ft (60cm) tall. Hardy to 10°F (−12°C), US zones 8–10.

Bidens

Bidens ferulifolia This short-lived perennial, usually grown as an annual, is native to the southern United States and Mexico. It grows up to 12in (30cm) tall and has fern-like, bright green foliage. From midsummer to autumn it bears starry, golden yellow flowers, 1¼–1½ (3–4cm) wide, or larger in the cultivar **'Golden Goddess'** pictured here. *Bidens ferulifolia* has a rambling habit, making it ideal for ground-cover and edging, and for all types of containers. It will grow in any zone but will be killed by the first hard frost.

PLANTING HELP   Sow seed indoors in warmth in spring. Plant out seedlings after hardening off and when all risk of frost is past. It needs moist, well-drained soil and a position in full sun.

Rudbeckia hirta 'Rustic Dwarfs'

Rudbeckia hirta 'Becky Mixed'

Black-eyed Susan *Rudbeckia hirta*

DAHLIAS

Dahlias with blue *Salvia uliginosa* at Hidcote

Dahlia 'Showpiece Mixed'

Dahlia 'David Howard'

Dahlia 'Red Rigoletto'

Dahlia 'Moon Fire'

Dahlia 'Bishop of Llandaff' with red pansies and the yellow spires of *Ligularia* at Bosvigo House, Truro

Dahlia

The familiar dahlias seen in our gardens are complex hybrids derived from *Dahlia pinnata* and *Dahlia coccinea*, both native to Mexico and Central America. These species were introduced to Europe at the end of the 18th century. Much of the early breeding took place in Mexican and French gardens and now there are perhaps 20,000 cultivars. They are tuberous-rooted perennials that grow up to 4ft (1.2m) tall, whose tubers are lifted for the winter. Annual bedding dahlias, such as **'Showpiece Mixed'** and the delicate 'Mignon Silver' (*not illustrated*), are more compact and may be raised from seed. There is also great variety in flower style and they are classified into several groups, of which the main ones are: Pompon, Cactus, Decorative, Collerette, Anemone-flowered and Single.

PLANTING HELP   Bedding dahlias are raised from seed sown in a greenhouse at 60°F (15°C) and hardened off before planting out when all risk of frost is past. Those grown from tubers should be planted out at the same time. They are not frost-hardy and the tubers are lifted in autumn, just after the first frosts touch the foliage. The tubers are kept in dry sand or peat in a cool but frost-free place for the winter. They enjoy a fertile soil rich in humus and should have a sunny position.

Cactus-type dahlias

French and African marigolds with *Senecio cineraria* 'Cirrus' and *Cordyline*

French marigold 'Favourite'

Tagetes tenuifolia 'Golden Gem'

Tagetes

A small genus native to central and southern America, mostly with pinnately divided leaves. Tagetes includes three important types of marigold, all of which were first introduced to Europe at the end of the 18th century. Hardy to 20°F (−6°C), US zones 9–10.

PLANTING HELP Seeds of all types of marigold are sown in warmth in early spring, or outside in late spring. They like a fairly fertile, well-drained soil and a sunny position. Young plants may be damaged by slugs, while the flowers of African marigolds may rot in the middle in wet weather. Regular dead-heading in the summer will prolong the display.

African Marigolds These are upright plants 12–30in (30–75cm) tall, with large fully double, cream or light yellow to orange flower heads up to 5in (12cm) wide from late spring to early autumn. There are many named forms, from the tall 'Crackerjack Mixed', with large yellow to orange flowers, to the compact 'Inca Mixed', 10in (25cm) tall with very large flowers. Derived from *Tagetes erecta*.

French Marigolds These have smaller flowers in shades of yellow, orange and deep mahogany red and are bred from *Tagetes patula*. They are compact and bushy, seldom exceeding 10in (25cm) tall, with flowers about 2in (5cm) wide.

FRENCH & AFRICAN MARIGOLDS

French marigold 'Jolly Jester'

French marigold
'Mahogany Red'

African marigolds at the Villa Pallavicino

The Boy Series grows to 6in (15cm), with double flowers ranging from yellow to deep orange; taller is 'Tiger Eyes' at 12in (30cm), with deep red outer petals and a central button of bright yellow. Afro-French marigolds are hybrids between these two groups, and are intermediate in character.

Signet Marigolds   These are derived from *Tagetes tenuifolia* and make erect bushy plants to 12in (30cm) tall, with single flowers 1in (2.5cm) wide in summer and autumn. In the **Gem** Series, such as '**Golden Gem**', they range from lemon-yellow to deep orange, while 'Starfire' may be orange, yellow or red, and sometimes bicolored. They make good edging for borders.

African marigold 'Vanilla'

Cosmos 'Purity' with *Lavatera* 'Barnsley' at Cockermouth in October

Cosmos 'Pied Piper'

Cosmos 'Imperial Pink'

Cosmos

Cosmos bipinnatus The wild Cosmos grows to 6ft (1.8m) tall with daisy-type flowers, 3in (8cm) wide, throughout the summer. Its leaves are divided into may fine lobes and contrast beautifully with the large flowers. *Cosmos bipinnatus* is available in many selected forms, varying in height and in shades of pink, lilac and white. 'Sonata' (*not illustrated*) is a shorter, bushier variety than most that grows to 20in (50cm). **'Imperial Pink'** is one of the more striking forms available. **'Pied Piper'** has tubular florets. *Cosmos bipinnatus* is native to Mexico and the southern United States and was introduced to Europe at the end of the 18th century. Hardy to 32°F (0°C), US zone 10 or slightly lower. It is vigorous, easily grown in most gardens and is good for cutting.

PLANTING HELP Seeds may be planted in a greenhouse in early spring and hardened off before planting out in late spring. Alternatively, seed can be planted outside in late spring *in situ*. Plant about 18in (45cm) apart. *Cosmos bipinnatus* prefers a sunny, sheltered position, reasonable soil and average rainfall. It may be prone to attack by aphids, botrytis and slugs. Dead-heading will encourage flowering to continue into the autumn.

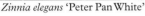

Zinnia elegans 'Peter Pan White'

Zinnia elegans 'Fantastic Light Pink' at Longwood

Zinnia

Native to Mexico where they were cultivated by the Aztecs. Wild *Zinnia* species have large red, orange or yellow flowers, but modern varieties range from green to white and purple, and from giant doubles to miniature pompons. They are fine showy plants for containers or the open border.

***Zinnia elegans* cultivars**   These grow 8–30in (20–75cm) tall and flower in summer and early autumn. The **Fantastic** and **Peter Pan** series are dwarf selections in various colours. The Ruffles series is one of the taller selections, the long-stemmed flowers being suitable for cutting.

Zinnia haageana (syn. *Z. angustifolia*) and **cultivars**   These also come in a range of heights and colours, flowering in summer only. They can be grown in any zone but will be killed off by the first frost.

Zinnia elegans 'Torch'

PLANTING HELP   Zinnias dislike root disturbance, so are best planted out from pot-grown seedlings where they are to flower. The seed can be sown from May to early June, when the soil and weather have warmed up. They will grow in any well-drained soil and like a position in full sun. If required, they can be started off indoors in March and April. Sow seeds in individual pots and keep warm, 75–80°F (24–27°C), and moist but not over-wet. The seedlings should be hardened off gradually and planted out carefully after all risk of frost has passed. Dead-heading will prolong the flowering period.

Zinnia haageana 'Persian Carpet'

Index

INDEX

INDEX